NEVER SETTLE

Leading With A **Daring Vision, Plan** And **Winning Mindset**

ARON MARQUEZ

Copyright © 2020 by Aron Marquez.

All rights reserved.
Printed in the United States of America.

No part of this publication may be reproduced or distributed in any form or any means, without the prior permission of the publisher. Requests for permission should be directed to permissions@indiebooksintl.com, or mailed to Permissions, Indie Books International, 2424 Vista Way, Suite 316, Oceanside, CA 92054.

Neither the publisher nor the author is engaged in rendering legal or other professional services through this book. If expert assistance is required, the services of appropriate professionals should be sought. The publisher and the author shall have neither liability nor responsibility to any person or entity with respect to any loss or damage caused directly or indirectly by the information in this publication.

The Salvation Army logo is a registered trademark of The Salvation Army USA.
The Golden Arches logo is a registered trademark by McDonald's Corporation.

ISBN: 978-1-952233-28-9
Library of Congress Control Number: 2020918959

Designed by Joni McPherson, mcphersongraphics.com

INDIE BOOKS INTERNATIONAL, INC®
2424 VISTA WAY, SUITE 316
OCEANSIDE, CA 92054
www.indiebooksintl.com

This book is dedicated to the people who made Wildcat Oil Tools' success possible: my family, our employees, and our customers. I thank each of you for your help and I look forward to our next chapter together.

TABLE OF CONTENTS

Introduction vii
Chapter One: Introduction To Visionary Leadership 1
Chapter Two: Defining Visionary Leadership. 9
Chapter Three: Childhood Biography 25
Chapter Four: Wildcat Oil Tools' Start. 35
Chapter Five: Mindset 53
Chapter Six: Wildcat Oil Tools' Growth, US Locations 73
Chapter Seven: Wildcat Oil Tools' International Growth 85
Chapter Eight: Wildcat Oil Tools' Growth In Products And Services. 97
Chapter Nine: Vision Discipline And Executing The Plan 105
Chapter Ten: Getting The Right Team 125
Chapter Eleven: Communication 139
Chapter Twelve: Responding To Adversity 153
Chapter Thirteen: Ethics. 171
Chapter Fourteen: Never Stand Still. 183
Chapter Fifteen: Personal Habits. 199
Chapter Sixteen: Encouraging Initiative 219
Chapter Seventeen: Branding 225
Conclusion 237
About the Author 239
Acknowledgments. 241

INTRODUCTION

The idea for this book came from a simple question that I was often asked. How did I grow Wildcat Oil Tools from a start-up company with four pieces of rental equipment, two family members for employees, and no actual location that we could call our own, to an international service company with hundreds of employees, products, and services in just a few years? I would answer that I wasn't the reason for Wildcat's growth. That growth came from a Vision to make Wildcat Oil Tools a top-flight, international service company, a superior management team, and a solid Implementation Plan. I furnished the Vision, recruited the team, and supported their efforts to develop and implement a Plan for success. Collectively, we grew and developed Wildcat Oil Tools until it became a top-flight, international service company.

This response invariably led to further questions about my Vision and Wildcat's Implementation Plan. That discussion often led to the suggestion that I write a book explaining this process so that others could follow our example. I was always flattered that people thought Wildcat's experience was worthy of a book, but I'd laugh off the suggestion because there weren't enough hours in the day to accomplish everything that I needed to attend to, let alone write a book. As we grew, however, and Wildcat Oil Tools' management team began assuming more operational control, the thought of writing a book germinated until it seemed like a good idea; so I embarked on this process.

While writing this book, I came to realize there was another critically important factor in our success: our Mindset. I knew our people made Wildcat Oil Tools' success possible and I had assumed this was because we recruited the right people. We did, but I've come to realize it wasn't because we recruited talented people. Hiring good people is critical to your success, but businesses with good people working for them fail every day. Wildcat succeeded because a group of talented people were relentless in their pursuit of a goal. My senior staff bought into the Vision of making Wildcat Oil Tools a top-flight international service company and committed themselves to our Implementation Plan. Their commitment, along with an unrelenting determination to succeed, effectively became a self-fulfilling prophecy.

Vision, Plan, Mindset. You're going to see these three concepts discussed repeatedly in this book because they work. With apologies to my English teachers, I'm capitalizing Vision, Plan, and Mindset throughout this book to emphasize the three keys to visionary leadership. They explain our success and more importantly, they'll work for you and your organization.

Aron Marquez

CHAPTER ONE

INTRODUCTION TO VISIONARY LEADERSHIP

Imagine you've been talked into parachuting for reasons that you can no longer remember, and you're now moments away from leaving a perfectly good airplane in midair. You're sitting on the floor of the plane, decked out with a parachute, a reserve chute, and a helmet. Your parachute straps are incredibly uncomfortable. In fact, the straps around your upper thighs are rubbing so hard that you're starting to wonder if you should loosen them, but that small part of your mind that isn't screaming, "You aren't going to do this, are you?" tells you that it would probably be a bad idea to loosen anything attached to your parachute.

Someone opens the plane door and a rush of air hits you in the face like a bucket of ice water. You look outside, and all you see is wide-open blue sky. Then, like an executioner coming to open a cell door for the final time, the jump instructor crawls over to you. He's smiling as he starts tugging and shaking your chute, harness, and helmet. It's all you can do not to fall over. When he stops shaking, you take a quick look. Fortunately, nothing appears to have come loose but the fact that parachuting isn't something you're going to do, it's something you're about to do *right now* hits home. You're seriously considering telling the instructor that you've changed your mind but when you open your mouth, nothing comes out. The instructor leans over and yells in your ear as he connects your static line, "You're good; enjoy the ride!" He then positions you in the door—some might say forcibly shoves—before he shouts, "Go!" and gives you a not-so-gentle push.

You're falling and even though your eyes are truly wide open, you can't see anything beyond a blue blur. The wind is howling in your ears—or is that you screaming? Suddenly there's a tug on your harness and everything slows down. You look up. Mercifully, your chute is open and you're gently falling. Everything slows down and you realize you're still alive! Your heart has slowed down to a gentle ninety-nine beats a minute and your blood pressure is now probably low enough that it can be measured. Everything has become peaceful. The view is breathtaking and it's amazingly quiet. All you can hear is the gentle flapping of the edge of your parachute. Wait! Is it supposed to do that? Before you can panic, you see a bird flying below you. That's so cool. This must be what heaven is like. Wouldn't it be cool if you were a bird and could do this anytime you wanted?

Your time in nirvana is interrupted by a voice coming from the earplugs you'd forgotten about. Someone on the ground is telling you that you look good and is reminding you that they'll talk you through the landing. Oh my God, the landing! You try to remember what your instructor said about how to land, but the ground is coming up awfully fast and your mind goes back into overdrive. Wasn't there something about positioning yourself so that you were headed into

CHAPTER 1

the wind? Or was it downwind? Which way is the wind blowing? Where's the landing zone? Boy, the ground's coming up fast!

A calm, confident voice starts giving you instructions. "Turn right until you're headed to the water tower. Okay, straighten up. Turn right again until you're lined up with the flagpole at the end of the landing zone. Hold it. A little left. Hold it. Look straight ahead. Okay, pull both toggles!" Your mind can barely process the commands because of adrenaline overload, but somehow you manage to pull on the toggles. Just as you do, your feet touch the ground and you try to run as you were instructed, but you trip and fall face-forward. Fortunately, the landing zone has nice grass. You know that because you've got some in your mouth, your nose, and one ear. Thankfully, your parachute lands on top of you, so no one can see your sunglasses spread across your face or how much dirt and grass you managed to ingest.

You start to pick yourself up and then you realize, you jumped out of an airplane! It doesn't matter that you didn't exactly nail the landing. Nobody got that on video, did they? No matter, you just did something that most people only dream about and even if they say that only an idiot would jump out of a perfectly good airplane, they still secretly dream about it. You, however, aren't limited to living life through your dreams; instead you're a doer, and for the rest of your life, you'll be able to look back at this accomplishment with a sense of pride.

Starting your own business is a similar experience. It can be scary because it's risky. When you're an employee, there's a certain amount of security. You know you'll get a regular paycheck even if the business had a bad month. You work in an office or building for which you didn't have to sign a lease. Your name isn't on a business loan that must be repaid even if the business fails. On the other hand, when you're the owner, nothing's guaranteed. If the business makes money, so do you. If it doesn't, you don't either, but you still have to make payroll. If your business is small and just starting, it's your name on the bank note, the lease, and every credit application. And if your business fails, everyone will look to you for repayment.

There is also the risk of embarrassment. When you're the owner, you're responsible for everything and if you fail—and most start-ups do—there will be no place to hide. The fact that your business failed will be with you forever. However, just as being willing to take the risk to jump out of a plane separates you from the herd, successfully building a business is something that few are even willing to risk trying and so when you pull it off, it's an accomplishment that you can be proud of for the rest of your life.

There's absolutely nothing like successfully building a business. There are the financial rewards that come from assuming the financial risk and it's definitely rewarding to look around at a thriving business and say to yourself, "I built this." However, it's also a way to make a positive difference. People need jobs and most of the jobs in the US are created by small businesses. The day you become an employer will be one of the scariest days of your life because you now have a payroll to make every single pay period, but it will also be one of the most rewarding days of your life.

When you give a person a job, you make a difference in their lives. Their paycheck allows them to provide for their families which, in turn, gives them a better sense of worth and provides a feeling of security for their families. But beyond that, you give an

CHAPTER 1

individual a chance to grow by learning new skills or handling greater responsibility. For most people, a large part of our identity is associated with our work. Provide an individual with an opportunity to work with good people and for an organization that they can be proud of, and you've improved their self-image.

To start and build a business, or any other type of organization successfully, you must be a leader. My intent with this book is to make you a better leader by showing how to lead with a Vision. This book illustrates visionary leadership in a business setting, and it describes how we at Wildcat Oil Tools took a Vision and used an Implementation Plan and a collective unrelenting Mindset to achieve a business goal. Although I rely primarily on business examples to make my point, this discussion is applicable to any leadership situation, and it's particularly applicable to any personal challenges that you will face as a leader.

Before we go any further, let's consider what, exactly, is visionary leadership and is this a skill that can be learned or developed? Dictionaries tell us that "leadership" is the action of leading a group of people or an organization to accomplish a common goal. Intuitively we know what that definition means, and we have no trouble identifying a leader when we see one in action. However, identifying someone as a good leader before they take over an organization and prove themselves is more difficult. The problem is as old as history itself. If you had been on Pharaoh's court or an Egyptian living in Cairo, would you have recognized Moses as a leader before the Red Sea split?

Leadership is no less important today than it was in Moses's time. Organizations of every type and size are constantly searching for better leaders. This quest is in large part because we typically attribute an organization's successes to good leadership and its failures to bad. A football team has a good season and we give the coach a raise and a new contract; but if the team struggles, fans scream for change. The same thing happens in the boardroom. A publicly-traded company exceeds Wall Street's earnings expectations and we heap praise on the chief executive officer (CEO) and senior management team; but if the company fails to meet those expectations, shareholders and financial reporters begin grumbling about the CEO. If earnings don't improve, the company hires a new CEO.

Some will debate whether leaders are born or made. I firmly believe they are made. Undoubtedly, some people are born with the skills that predispose them to be good coaches, business leaders, or elected officials. However, if you ask yourself who are the top three to five leaders that you know of, regardless of whether their fields were business, politics, or sports, I'll bet that for each of these individuals, you'll find defining moments that led them to become a leader—such as Moses and the burning bush—and that their leadership skills developed over time.

I'm not alone in believing that leadership skills can be developed. Every year, the US military and multi-national corporations spend millions of dollars training their people to become better leaders. Colleges and universities across the country offer numerous leadership courses. Private groups offer any number of seminars and training programs on leadership skills. I can't believe so many people and organizations would spend that much time, money, and effort on leadership training if it didn't work.

CHAPTER 1

I'll use the example of Wildcat Oil Tools' growth from a small oilfield service firm with three employees, four pieces of rental equipment, and a humble location into a multi-national energy services company with a long list of products and services to illustrate the concept of leading an organization with a Vision, Plan, and Mindset. You can use our example and the lessons that we learned to improve your organization regardless of its type or field because when a group of people are motivated and equipped to fulfill a Vision, they will accomplish wonders. I also want to enable you to better realize your own potential. You can do that by adopting better personal habits and by putting the power of your mind to work for you. Everyone knows eating better and exercising are good for you, but too few people realize they're not putting their most powerful tool—their minds—to work for them. I'll show you how.

CHAPTER TWO

DEFINING VISIONARY LEADERSHIP

At its core, visionary leadership is motivating and equipping a group of people to collectively work toward achieving an aspirational goal. Individually, each of us is capable of motivating ourselves and each of us should do the things necessary to make sure that we are self-disciplined and are maximizing our personal potential. Organizations, however, need leaders to reach their potential. A motivated individual is a great thing because a motivated individual will always outperform their peers. But an organization full of highly-motivated people who aren't on the same page is a disaster. On the other hand, if you can orient those individuals to the same goal, you can take on the world.

Along with sharing Wildcat Oil Tools stories, I'm going to use a mythical steakhouse in your community to illustrate some of my points. We'll assume that you're the owner and general manager of this steakhouse and that you have a Vision: to operate the best steakhouse in town. What constitutes the best can be debated, but let's assume your Vision is to have the most popular fine-dining steakhouse in town. It's the place people go to when they want a prime cut of steak, outstanding service, and an exceptional atmosphere.

If you have the best head waiter in town, you've got an advantage over the competition. Similarly, if you've got the best business manager and the best chef in town you've got an advantage. That advantage, however, is diminished if each of the three has a different picture of what the steakhouse should look like and how it should operate. For example, your business manager is focused strictly on lowering costs to achieve a more efficient operation and wants to purchase lower-cost cuts of meat. The head waiter wants to increase the average cost of a ticket and to increase the nightly table turnover, so he prioritizes training time over techniques to encourage people to order appetizers and dessert and providing customers their check in a timely manner when they've finished their meal. The chef's priority is to diversify the menu by including a revolving list of specials from around the world. Individually, each of these priorities is fine, but none is consistent with the others, let alone with your Vision. Imagine if all three had the same Vision you do of what the restaurant should be and they were collectively working together to make this Vision a reality. Not only would they stop working at cross purposes, but by working collectively, they'd magnify your talent advantage.

When it comes to an organization, the whole truly is greater than the sum of its parts. You get three talented individuals working toward the same aspirational goal and suddenly your steakhouse is running like a finely-tuned, high-performance engine. Their talent and creativity are focused, they're putting peer pressure on each other to accomplish the same goal, and they're setting an example for everyone else. That synergy gives you such a competitive advantage over the other restaurants in town that you might start feeling sorry for your competition.

I know from my personal experience that visionary leadership works and that it will take your organization much further than anyone now thinks is possible. A word of warning, however: it requires a lot of effort on your part. You must have a compelling Vision, a realistic Implementation Plan, and an unrelenting Mindset to succeed. You must sell the Vision and Plan to your organization and have the self-discipline to stick to the Plan long after the initial excitement has worn off. Your Mindset must be strong enough to withstand the inevitable problems that will arise. I know it can be done, because I saw it happen at Wildcat Oil Tools.

To demonstrate what visionary leadership is, I offer three examples of visionary leaders: Henry Ford, George Washington, and Vince Lombardi. Before I go further, please understand that I do not regard myself the equal of any of these gentlemen, I do not consider that what we accomplished at Wildcat Oil Tools is comparable to their achievements, and I do not believe you must try to emulate anyone of them to be a successful visionary leader. I use them because each is a clear example of visionary leadership at work and when you consider their stories, you will understand what I mean when I say visionary leadership. I also use them because each illustrates how the right Mindset empowers individuals and groups to achieve great things.

I've intentionally selected leaders from different eras, responsible for different types of organizations, and with distinctly different personalities to illustrate my point that visionary leadership works and that you can apply it within your organization regardless of whether it is a business, non-profit, athletic team, church, or political campaign. None of these three individuals was perfect. Washington, for example, owned slaves and Ford fought union organization with brutal intimidation tactics. However, each leader was unquestionably transformative and each had a Vision that others believed in and followed.

Henry Ford didn't invent the automobile or the assembly line. He did, however, introduce innovation to the automobile industry by manufacturing a car that middle-class Americans could afford, and, in the process, he revolutionized travel. He accomplished this with a Vision: build a car for the masses. In Henry Ford's biography, *My Life and Work* (New York: Doubleday and Company, 1922), Ford described the Vision he presented to his staff as:

"I will build a motor car for the great multitude. It will be large enough for the family but small enough for the individual to run and care for. It will be constructed of the best materials by the best men to be hired, after the simplest designs that modern engineering can devise. But it will be so low in price that no man making a good salary will be unable to own one—and enjoy with his family the blessings of hours of pleasure in God's great open spaces."

Ford's unwavering pursuit of this Vision, and his ability to sell it, ultimately lead to the creation of the Ford Motor Company, and then to the manufacture of cars such as the Model T.

Ford would become one of the wealthiest men in America, but he came from a humble background. He was born and raised on his father's farm in Michigan. He left the farm in 1879 to become

CHAPTER 2

an apprentice at the Michigan Car Company, a railroad car manufacturer. Ford returned to his family's farm in 1882, where he operated and serviced the portable steam engines used by farmers. In 1891, he moved to Detroit and worked as a night engineer for the Edison Electric Illuminating Company. Within a few years, he rose to become Edison Electric's chief engineer. This, however, was not his only pursuit. After work, Ford and some friends developed horseless carriages. In 1896, they built the Quadricycle, which had four wheels that looked like heavy bicycle wheels and was steered with a tiller. They built a second, more sophisticated vehicle in 1898.

Ford then manifested his ability to lead by Vision and his unrelenting pursuit of that Vision. Despite his lack of experience and the risks inherent in a start-up company engaged in a new technology, he convinced a group of businessmen to back him by funding a company to make and sell automobiles. Ford's lack of business experience lead to inevitable mistakes and the company failed. So, too, did his second company. Ford, however, never wavered from his Vision to develop a car for the masses. He started building and driving racing cars. The success of his racing cars attracted investors and in 1903 he incorporated his third automobile company: Ford Motor Company.

The Ford Motor Company succeeded for a variety of reasons. In addition to attracting investors, Ford identified and recruited outstanding people and he sold them on his Vision. Their first car was the now-famous Model A. In 1906, their Model N became the best-selling car in America. The Model N sold for $600. By today's standards, that sounds incredibly inexpensive, but in 1906 most Americans couldn't afford to purchase one.

Ford remained committed to his Vision of building a car for the masses. Despite pressure from investors to concentrate on a more luxurious car, he and a hand-picked group of employees developed the Model T, which was introduced on October 1, 1908. It was easy to operate, maintain, and handle on rough roads. It was also an instant success.

Ford's Vision and Mindset drove the company to improve the Model T and, equally important, to lower its cost so that more Americans could own one. Ford's commitment to lowering costs and his ability to sell this commitment to his employees was critical. Every manufacturer strives to lower costs. All things being equal, when a manufacturer lowers its costs, profits increase. But it's one thing to try to motivate an employee to lower costs so that the company's owners can make more money. It's another to motivate employees to lower costs so that more Americans can afford to own an automobile. Which would motivate you more, increasing the boss's profits or helping more Americans to own a car?

Ford's Vision to make automobiles affordable for the masses can be seen throughout the company's subsequent decisions and innovations. The Ford Motor Company moved into a large plant in 1910 and developed a moving assembly line. At first, Ford faced labor issues because people objected to the repetitive nature of assembly line work. But he overcame that with a higher wage, $5 a day, that allowed workers to buy the car they were helping build. Later, a larger plant was built on the Rouge River. This location allowed for the delivery of raw materials by railroad and steamer. The new factory not only constructed cars but many of their components such as steel, glass, and tires. Each of these factors made the factory more efficient and, therefore, lowered the cost to construct a new car.

Ford's Vision, his ability to sell that Vision to investors and employees, and his unrelenting pursuit of that Vision, revolutionized not only transportation and manufacturing but society as well. Many others followed his example and constructed their own factories with assembly lines. This development led to the migration of large numbers of people from farms to the cities. The higher wages these individuals could earn from factory jobs, along with their ability to purchase lower-cost consumer goods, led to the creation of the middle class as we know it today.

———

George Washington is commonly referred to as the Father of our country and with good reason. Interestingly, several of his contemporaries were better positioned to hold this role. Benjamin Franklin and Thomas Jefferson were better educated and both had more international experience. John Adams was more intelligent. John Hancock was a better communicator. Others had more military experience. Believe it or not, even though he is one of our country's most famous military leaders, prior to his appointment as head of the Continental Army, Washington had never commanded a large army in the field. His military inexperience lead to several critical mistakes. For example, in 1776, his army was nearly destroyed in New York because he allowed it to be flanked and become caught between the British Army and the East River. Washington's army survived because of a providential fog that allowed Washington to ferry his troops to Manhattan secretly without losing a man. In fact, even though we think of Washington as a great general, he actually lost more battles than he won.

Washington was, however, a visionary leader. He had a Vision for a new nation in which free men governed themselves. By today's standards, one can challenge this statement because in America's early years, governance was left to landowning men, almost all of whom were white; but even so, in a world run by monarchies with limited due process protections for individuals, Washington's Vision was truly revolutionary. Furthermore, the Constitution that came out of the War of Independence created the foundation for democracy as we know it today.

Visions often involve risk because they represent a significant change from the status quo. Fortunately, Washington was a risk-taker. When he accepted his commission as Commander of the Continental Army, he put his life and possessions at risk. Had the revolution failed, at best Washington would have lost all of his possessions and spent the rest of his life in prison. It's quite possible that he would have been executed. Washington also took several risks as Commanding General. For example, during the winter encampment at Valley Forge, he had all his soldiers inoculated against smallpox infection. I realize your reaction to this may be, "So?" In the 1770s, however, inoculations were new and risky, and smallpox was particularly dangerous.

We think of a soldier's greatest risk as being killed or wounded in battle; however, Colonial and British soldiers were far more likely to die from disease than from an enemy musket. Washington's army was never large and early in the war, smallpox devastated it. Consequently, when Washington took the Colonial Army to Valley

CHAPTER 2

Forge in 1777, he had ample reason to be more fearful of a smallpox epidemic than an attack by the British.

Valley Forge was a low point in the war because Washington had just lost control of Philadelphia, the nation's capital, due to leadership mistakes, and the Colonial Army was being forced to winter in an area that the British had recently burned. Disease and desertion were rapidly depleting an army that couldn't afford to lose any more men. Inoculations were relatively new and were particularly risky because doctors gave their patients a mild case of smallpox. Consequently, even when the inoculation was successful, the patient was incapacitated for several days. Washington weighed the risks and correctly decided the benefit of a healthy army outweighed the inoculation risk. Fortunately, the British were unaware of the inoculation program. Had they attacked in the days after the inoculations, the Continental Army would have been unable to defend itself. The British could have walked in and captured the Continental Army with little effort.

It was one thing for Washington to take a personal risk, but we remember him today because he led others to do so. Even beyond facing the best-trained and well-equipped army in the world, the Continental Army faced numerous and staggering challenges: limited military experience and training, inadequate supplies, and an inability to pay troops or reimburse officers for their expenses. Washington's conduct reveals an unrelenting Mindset in pursuit of a Vision. At the time, this Vision inspired his cold, sick, and hungry soldiers to look beyond the hopelessness of the present to a brighter future.

Today we would say Washington walked the talk. He served without pay and was nearly bankrupt at the war's end. Even so, in

1783, two years after the victory at Yorktown, when some of his officers threatened to overthrow the Continental Congress because they had not been paid, he appeared at a meeting of the officers and appealed to their sense of honor. During his remarks he reached into a pocket to retrieve a pair of glasses and theatrically remarked: "I have not only grown gray, but almost blind in service to my country." His display of self-sacrifice for a greater good squelched the potential rebellion in its tracks.

When the war was over, Washington could have easily assumed control of the country and, under the norms of the time, would have been fully expected to do so. History is full of military leaders who seized political power during times of revolution: Julius Caesar, Oliver Cromwell, Napoleon Bonaparte, and Mao Zedong. However, Washington, who repeatedly affirmed his commitment to civilian rule during the war, publicly surrendered his commission to a grateful Congress at the end of the war. When King George III heard Washington intended to do this, he remarked, "If he does that, he will be the greatest man in the world." Today, we take the transfer of power from one administration to another for granted. In the eighteenth century, however, it was essentially unprecedented. At that time, power was normally transferred only after a bloodbath. We can thank Washington's commitment to his Vision for the freedom that we enjoy to elect our own political leaders and the ability we have to replace those leaders at the next election.

Vince Lombardi is known as one of the best coaches to ever work in the National Football League (NFL). When he was young, however, he wanted to be a priest. Lombardi changed his mind when he became an exceptional college football player at Fordham University. After college graduation, he became a college coach and then an assistant coach for the New York Giants. He helped the Giants win a league title in 1956. In 1959, he became the Green Bay Packers' head coach. Today, the Packers are a storied franchise, but in 1959, they were the worst team in the NFL. In two years, Lombardi made the Packers into the best team in football. He never had a losing season and when he retired, Lombardi had won five league championships and two Super Bowls.

Every NFL team has the same Vision: to win the Super Bowl, but each year, only one succeeds. Lombardi was successful because of his Mindset and his ability to convince his team to adopt that Mindset. Specifically, Lombardi convinced his teams they would win if they collectively and wholeheartedly followed his program of practices and game preparation. That might sound simplistic and obvious, but for most of us, until we successfully do something challenging, there will always be some doubt that it's possible. That doubt can be a self-fulfilling prophecy. Consider the four-minute mile. Today, even high-school runners occasionally run sub-four-minute miles. Until Roger Bannister broke the four-minute barrier in 1954, however, many considered it impossible because no one had ever done it. However, after Bannister showed it could be done, suddenly several others were able to do so as well. In fact, a year after Bannister's feat, three runners in a single race ran sub-four-minute miles. I seriously doubt their workouts changed; instead, they ran sub-four-minute miles because they believed they could.

The 1959 Packers had plenty of reasons to think that they were incapable of winning a championship regardless of how they practiced and prepared; and they had the benefit of several recent dismal seasons to illustrate their point. Lombardi first had to overcome this pessimism and to replace it with a winning Mindset. If you have a headache and I give you two aspirin, you expect them to make you feel better and I suspect this belief alone makes the aspirin more effective.

To instill a winning Mindset, Lombardi preached, demanded, and expected hard work from his teams. Hard work, however, is a universal constant in professional sports. Every professional coach encourages their players to work hard and every coach utilizes difficult practices, weight work, and conditioning to further this goal. What separated Lombardi from his peers was his ability to establish a team-wide commitment to his specific processes. Just as your belief in my aspirin helps your headache, the Packers' belief that Lombardi's program would work automatically made the program more effective. Their collective commitment created a winning Mindset that had been previously missing in Green Bay.

Lombardi sold his Vision by reaching his players on a personal level. He was a no-nonsense coach, but he was also passionate, energetic, and charismatic. He obviously wanted his players to improve so that the team's performance would improve; but he convinced his players he also wanted them to improve because he cared about them as individuals. Consequently, when he was tough on his players, they saw it as his effort to improve them personally because he believed in them and saw their potential. Just as your father gave you the confidence to do something scary when you were young by saying, "You've got this," Lombardi gave his players the belief that they could become exceptional if they trusted him. Lombardi's enthusiasm was contagious. Soon his players were committed and the team was united.

Lombardi knew hard work alone was insufficient because every NFL team works hard. Each team has a strenuous conditioning program, practices long hours, and prepares extensively for their opponents. Lombardi knew his teams had to execute better than their opponents if they wanted to be champions; therefore, Lombardi preached perfection and a commitment to each other. When Lombardi's players started believing they could win, and they committed themselves to his process and each other, the change was almost immediate. Players weren't simply going through the motions in practice; instead they worked with a purpose and they challenged and supported each other to do the same. That preparation resulted in better execution at game time, which further bolstered players' confidence and commitment. Ultimately, Lombardi's Packers became the best team in the NFL.

Washington, Ford, and Lombardi—three distinctive personalities who lived in three fundamentally different periods of time, who each faced significantly different challenges. All of them, however, accomplished unprecedented things because of their ability to lead with a Vision and a Mindset that didn't accept anything less than success. That same approach can work for you. This book relies heavily on my experience as CEO of Wildcat Oil Tools and my use of a Vision and Implementation Plan to grow Wildcat Oil Tools from almost nothing to an international oilfield service company. You shouldn't make the mistake of concluding that visionary leadership only works if you're in control of an organization. The techniques explained in this book will, if followed, make you a better leader regardless of your job or title.

Speaking of titles, all too often people assume leadership is attributed to a title and that without the right title, you can't be the leader. For example, if you're the CEO of an organization, then you're the leader, but if you're not the CEO, then you aren't. That's simply untrue. A title—or lack thereof—has nothing to do with leadership. Leadership is demonstrated through action and a lack of leadership is frequently manifested by a lack of action. Odds are that you've seen the situation where the person with the organization's premier title didn't actually lead the organization. A leader leads regardless of title. Consequently, you cannot let your title serve as an excuse for not leading, nor can you allow your title to become a substitute for your ability to lead.

In my opinion, titles are becoming increasingly unimportant. That same urge to give every kid who plays a participation trophy, which in the process devalues the winner's achievement, has led us to give everyone an impressive-sounding title. Consequently, I don't pay much attention to an individual's title. I do, however, pay a lot of attention to their actions. In this book, I'll share stories of frontline people at Wildcat—in other words, people without a fancy title but who were knowledgeable, dedicated, and hardworking—who had some of the best ideas that we've ever used. I'll also share the things that I do to make sure everyone is heard. I listen to Wildcat's employees for several reasons, including to make sure I don't miss a great idea because I've let someone's title or label blind me to their insight.

CHAPTER 2

Now that you know what a visionary leader is, I'm going to take a step back to explain how Wildcat Oil Tools and I reached this point. In the process, I'll show you how Vision, Plan, and Mindset worked for us and how to use all three for yourself.

CHAPTER THREE

CHILDHOOD BIOGRAPHY

My personal story is a collection of coincidences and ironies. For example, my Vision for Wildcat Oil Tools can be traced back to my early childhood years, even though my family had no oilfield connection and I didn't start working in the oil and gas industry until I was in college. I should also point out that when I started Wildcat Oil Tools, not only did my Vision and Implementation Plan not exist, at the time I had no intention of running an oilfield service company. It wasn't that I hadn't thought about it: after college I worked for a large service company for several years and when I left that company, I fully intended to transition to something else. Wildcat's start was the unintended consequence of a bad investment. But before I get to that, let me share my personal story.

I was born in Ojinaga, a small, rural town in northern Mexico, in the state of Chihuahua, across the Rio Grande from Presidio, Texas. The opportunities in Ojinaga are limited and, unfortunately, too many are tied to cross-border drug trafficking. My parents are honest, hardworking individuals who wanted no part of drug trafficking. They made sure that every one of their four kids knew better than to tread down that path.

Because my parents refused to engage in illegal activity, and because the local employment opportunities were limited, my father had to travel to the US for work and my mom held down two jobs to make ends meet. My parents' work schedules prevented them from spending as much time with us as they would have liked. Fortunately, my grandmother helped fill the void. She, too, believed in honest work and she helped instill that attitude in me, my brother, and two sisters. Between my parents and my grandmother, we were never hungry or without guidance. Thanks to their examples, we all knew beyond any doubt that having a good work ethic was non-negotiable and that whatever we ended up doing, it wouldn't involve drug trafficking or other illegal activity.

The importance of this lesson cannot be understated. We've all heard of people who were born into wealth, who fell into success, or who won the lottery. It's sometimes fun to dream about receiving such a windfall. Every visionary leader that I've known, however, led by example. If you want your people to follow you, they must respect you, and that respect must be earned. That means that a leader must visibly work as hard, if not harder, than anyone else in the organization and that when challenges hit, the leader must have an unshakeable determination to succeed. If that's not you, then you should probably put this book down. On the other hand, if you're driven to succeed, if you don't mind getting your hands dirty, and if the thought of quitting repulses you, keep reading. I'll show you how to put those talents to work.

CHAPTER 3

Growing up in Mexico is understandably different than growing up in the US. For example, Ojinaga schools were so limited in resources that students' textbooks didn't match. In other words, not every student in a classroom had the same book. Most of our books were passed down from universities to high schools and junior highs. Consequently, our teachers had a collection of books. This lack of textbooks meant that they couldn't tell the class to turn to page eighty-nine, nor give everyone the same reading assignment. Instead, your homework assignment depended on which book you had. We had dedicated teachers who cared, but their lack of resources limited what they could do. At the time, I didn't know any better, so it wasn't a concern; but as I looked back later, I knew this state of affairs wasn't right, and I was determined to make sure my family had better resources.

Children in Mexico entertain themselves in different ways than American kids do. None of my friends had an expensive video gaming system. Instead, we played soccer on a dirt field. I loved soccer. My friends and I played every night until it got dark. These games were an important part of my development. Soccer, much more so than most sports, requires teamwork and creativity. Because we were not part of an organized league, we had to organize ourselves. Thus, not only did we exercise, we developed by learning how to work together and to resolve our own conflicts.

I feel like this self-reliance is an area where we had an advantage over many of the kids growing up in America. I understand why parents want to provide for their kids and I've seen my nieces and nephews enjoy a variety of organized activities. Sometimes, however, it's a good idea to turn off the television and game console, skip the organized play-date, and just go outside with a ball to play with your friends.

I was happy in Ojinaga. Then, one day my mom told us that we were moving to the US as soon as we received our permit. I started crying because I didn't want to leave Mexico. All my friends were there, my family was there, and my grandmother wasn't coming with us. My parents understood why I was upset, but because of the lack of opportunity, they also knew we couldn't live together as a family in Ojinaga. We eventually moved to Fort Stockton, Texas, a small, west Texas town between San Antonio and El Paso. Fort Stockton's economy is largely agricultural. There are several large ranches in the area, and it is also well known for onions. Those onions were instrumental in the development of my work ethic.

Our family worked all summer picking onions, which is dirty, backbreaking work. A tractor with a knife-like implement goes through the field first. The implement separates the onions from their roots and leaves them exposed on the surface. We would follow the tractor and pick up the onions. During the course of a day, that's a lot of walking, bending, lifting, and standing. We would get to the field at first light—actually it was still dark—to avoid some of the heat, but much of our work was still done in ninety-degree and sometimes even one-hundred-degree weather.

We pooled our earnings and my parents saved as much as possible. Our goal was to purchase a house. We didn't have enough money saved at the end of the summer, so when school started, we moved to Odessa, Texas to live with an aunt. I was in the fifth grade. We lived in South Odessa but because I spoke no English, I was assigned to an elementary school in North Odessa. My school

CHAPTER 3

experience was miserable. I was required to ride four buses to get from home to school, I had no friends, and I couldn't speak English. I was initially assigned to a bilingual class. The intent of a bilingual program is to transition students into English with instruction in both English and Spanish. It didn't take me long to realize I wouldn't learn English while attending class with students who were speaking Spanish almost exclusively and with teachers who were largely teaching in Spanish.

I asked my mom to have me transferred to a regular class. She agreed and was able to have me switched. I struggled mightily in everything except math because I couldn't understand the teacher. To make matters worse, the other students laughed at my language difficulties. Fortunately, my crash course in English eventually paid off. I made some early friends by playing sports with classmates. That connection made me more comfortable and I started speaking English to them. They encouraged me and helped me with my English. I made my cousins in Odessa speak English to me. I struggled at first, but I gradually improved and by the end of the fifth grade I spoke passable English.

We returned to Fort Stockton to pick onions the summer after I completed the sixth grade. I hated getting up at three o'clock every morning and working until six o'clock every night. To this day, I can't stand the taste or smell of onions. By the end of the summer, I was completely sunburned, and I looked considerably worse for wear, but we were able to save enough money to buy a $25,000 house in Odessa.

I looked forward to school starting. No more getting up at 3 a.m. or spending all day in the onion fields, and I missed my friends. But one of the most embarrassing moments of my life occurred the first day of class. A teacher asked us to prepare a paper describing where we had gone on vacation that summer. We hadn't taken a vacation; my family and I had worked every day that summer. I was too embarrassed to say that, so I made up a story. No one ever figured out that my vacation story was fabricated, but at that age it hurt to feel left out. Everyone else was excited to share their story, and I was jealous of the fun that they'd had.

Junior high was, on the whole, a positive experience. I did well in school, we owned a house, and we were close enough to school that I could walk. I had several friends and was becoming more popular because I was good in sports. Dad was gone for work a lot, but my mother stayed at home and took care of everything.

We worked one more summer in the onion fields to earn money for furniture and holidays. At the end of the summer, my dad gave my brother and me $100 each with which to buy school clothes. I was so excited because until now, I had always worn hand-me-downs. I could finally buy what I wanted, and I knew what that was. I had seen a new pair of Polo boots. I loved those boots, so when my mother took us to the mall, I went straight to the store with the Polo boots. Unfortunately, the boots cost $150 and I only had $100. That's when I learned about layaway. I gave the saleswoman my $100 and she put the boots away for me.

I now had no money and no clothes, but I was two-thirds of the way to owning a great pair of Polo boots! I met my brother. He had managed to purchase shoes, pants, and shirts, and still had some money left over for food. He asked me where my clothes were. I told him, and he shook his head and said that Mom would kill me. He was

CHAPTER 3

almost right. My parents were furious. The next day I went to school wearing old clothes, but I knew what I wanted. I hustled and earned enough money to pay off my boots. I was proud of those boots both because I loved their look and because I had earned them. I've never regretted buying them.

Looking back, I understand my parents' frustration with me. They were thinking practically, and it certainly would have made sense for me to spend my money differently. However, I don't regret the decision because I knew what I wanted, and I put in the necessary work to get it. I'll discuss this distinction more later, but there is a tremendous difference between simply wanting something and being willing to earn it. I don't know a business owner who doesn't want their company to be successful. Unfortunately, I've seen too many who weren't willing to earn that success.

My early school experiences were also important because this is where I discovered that I wanted to be an entrepreneur. At the time, I wasn't sure what exactly I wanted to do. But I knew I wanted to be part of something special, something that depended on my talents rather than manual labor, and something that would allow me to see and experience more than west Texas. In short, I didn't want to be locked in with limited options and have my circumstances dictated to me. One year, a Junior Achievement group came to my school for a week to teach us about money, business ideas, and why people became entrepreneurs. Their program hit home for me. I knew that I wanted to become an entrepreneur and I immediately set out to do so.

We had an old lawnmower at home that occasionally worked. I asked my older brother Freddie to help me by fixing it so that I could use it to mow lawns. Freddie got the mower running and I started mowing yards for ten dollars, front and back. I quickly realized I had limited lawn-mowing talent. In fact, some of my former customers might say that I'm overstating my talent by describing it as limited. It was obvious that I would have to develop a different business strategy to keep my customers happy.

I learned that while I couldn't mow well, I enjoyed walking around the neighborhood meeting people. I had a friend, Julio, who was good at mowing yards but was shy. I started lining out yards to mow over the weekend. Julio mowed the yards and we split the proceeds. This arrangement worked well for both of us because it allowed each of us to focus on our strengths. This experience also confirmed my desire to become an entrepreneur when I grew up and increased my confidence that I could do so.

I've been an entrepreneur most of my adult life. Looking back, I can't imagine myself doing anything else. Fortunately, I live in a country that allows everyone an opportunity to succeed and, as I'll explain, I was given that chance. As I'll also explain, however, I'm grateful that it's also a country that allows you to fail, because otherwise the freedom to try would be severely curtailed and quite often limited to those with connections—which I didn't have.

As I said earlier, I knew I wanted to be part of something special. I had seen how hard my parents worked for everything and I had seen people who lived in much nicer homes and drove new cars and who didn't pick onions all summer. Selfishly, I wanted to be in the second group if for no other reason than to avoid onion-picking. Of equal importance, however, was my desire to have some control over my circumstances. My parents had instilled a work ethic in me. I knew that whatever I wanted, I had to earn. Thus, if I wanted to

CHAPTER 3

be part of something special, I'd have to do something to deserve it. Thanks to my parents, I knew beyond any doubt that I could and would do what it took to accomplish my dream.

I worked after school and during the summers while attending high school and paid a lot of my own expenses. I started college at Odessa Community College. I had a full-time job during the day and I went to school at night. There were times when the grind got old, but I knew quitting wasn't an option, so I held on to my dream and persevered. After two years at Odessa Community College, I attended the University of Connecticut where I majored in business. I learned a lot, and I got to see a different part of the country from west Texas. I transferred to Oklahoma University and obtained a BBA.

My first full time job was for a multi-national oil and gas service company. I was fortunate to have good mentors and I learned a lot about business in general and the oil and gas industry in particular. However, I never lost my dream to become an entrepreneur and so when I got a chance to start my own business, I took it.

My original business wasn't Wildcat Oil Tools; it was St. Andrews Royalties, a company that owned and managed mineral properties. St. Andrews still exists and is still active in the mineral business but since this book is about Wildcat Oil Tools, I'll leave that story for another day. Before I explain how Wildcat Oil Tools came to be, I have a question: What are you most passionate about? What would you like to see so badly that you're willing to focus your time and energy on it, and to take some personal risk to accomplish it? I ask this because visionary leadership requires a Vision to which you are passionately committed. You've heard the saying, "Everyone wants to be famous, but no one is willing to do the work to get there." The difference between "It'd be nice if I could" and "I'd crawl over broken glass to accomplish my goal" is the difference between success and mediocrity, if not failure. You cannot expect to sell others on a Vision if you're not committed to it yourself. Conversely, when you're around someone who is unashamedly excited about a project, you can't help but be excited yourself.

    I cannot understate the importance of finding a Vision about which you're passionate. Anything worth achieving will take time and effort and will involve ups and downs. People motivated by an "It'd be nice" attitude are unlikely to persevere; people willing to crawl over broken glass can weather the bad times. Your Vision is also important because the destination determines the route. What I mean is this: when you decide what you want to accomplish, you necessarily also start making decisions about how you'll do it. The opposite is also true: it makes no sense to worry about your intermediate steps until you have a destination in mind. How can you expect anyone to follow you if you're not sure where you're going or how you're going to get there?

CHAPTER FOUR

WILDCAT OIL TOOLS' START

As I noted at the beginning of this book, when people ask me about Wildcat Oil Tools' start and growth, I attribute our success to a Vision, an Implementation Plan, and a winning Mindset. Looking back, there is no question why we succeeded. Our Vision gave us a common goal, our Plan gave us a realistic way to achieve the Vision, and our Mindset ensured our commitment to the Vision even during the tough times. I should note, however, that none of these factors were present the day Wildcat Oil Tools opened for business.

I didn't start Wildcat Oil Tools with a grand Vision, let alone a Plan to achieve that Vision. In fact, at the time I had no interest in running a service company. I was approached by a close friend who asked me to loan his cousin $500,000 to purchase four Blow Out Preventers (BOPs). A BOP is a piece of pressure-control equipment that oil companies place on wells when working on them. A BOP allows the oil company to close the wellbore in an emergency to prevent it from blowing out. BOPs can also be used to add fluid to a wellbore or to control the volume of fluid to be withdrawn from a wellbore. My friend's cousin wanted to purchase four BOPs and then rent them to oil companies. He had a business Plan, but he needed capital.

I agreed to loan him the money and he purchased four brand-new BOPs. They were painted blue and they looked sharp. Unfortunately, my friend's cousin couldn't rent them. After several months I got anxious about my investment and I decided to end the relationship. I worked with my friend and his cousin and we reached an agreement. I cancelled the note in exchange for the four BOPs and a logo they had designed, which featured a wildcat.

I intended to sell the BOPs and recover as much of my investment as I could. My sister, however, convinced me that I should try to rent them instead because otherwise I'd lose a lot of my investment. Thus, Wildcat Oil Tools was launched. We had three employees—my father, my sister, and I; we also had four BOPs and a humble shop. My father helped at night and on weekends. My sister kept the books. My mother also pitched in. She sewed Wildcat logos on two of my shirts. (I still have one of those shirts.)

I've never been afraid to talk to people and ask them for work. So, just as in my lawn-mowing business days, I set out to find opportunities for my BOPs. I approached some friends at a local oil company, Fasken Oil and Ranch, and asked them if I could get a Master Service Agreement (MSA) with their company. An MSA is a contract that oil and gas companies enter into with their vendors. An MSA sets out the general terms and conditions that a vendor must satisfy when working for them. Most oil companies require a vendor to execute their MSA before being placed on their approved list of vendors. To get work for my BOPs, I needed to be on those lists.

CHAPTER 4

I started with a local company because they typically give their employees more flexibility when selecting vendors than larger companies. Most of the larger companies require vendors to have several years' experience and a documented safety record. Because Wildcat Oil Tools was a start-up company, we had no track record. Fortunately, my friends were willing to give me a shot. We entered into an MSA and they agreed to rent my BOPs. Wildcat Oil Tools was officially in business. By the way, I'm proud to say Fasken Oil and Ranch is still a Wildcat Oil Tools customer.

I was able to keep all four BOPs rented but I had to hustle and improvise to do so. Looking back, I can laugh at some of our solutions. We had no books, records, or billing process. I went to an office supply store and bought several carbonless, preprinted invoices—the kind where you write on the first page and your writing is copied onto the attached colored pages. When a customer called to rent a BOP, I'd fill out one of our invoices by hand and would take it and the BOP to the customer's well site. I'd get the customer to sign the invoice and I left the top copy with him. I'd take the remaining copies back to my sister to input into our books. Every now and then we ran into issues if I hadn't written firmly enough or clearly enough, or if something was laid on the top of the original invoice and it caused the other copies to become smudged. Overall, our customers were cooperative, and we worked through the problems one at a time.

BOPs are normally delivered to well sites on flatbed trailers. I had a pickup and a flatbed trailer. I could pull a trailer forward, but I couldn't back one up even if my life depended on it. Because of the risk involved, I didn't even try to back up a trailer when I was on a customer's location. If it was necessary to back up a trailer with our

BOP on it—and it invariably was—I'd talk someone into backing up my trailer for me. Oftentimes, I had to pay them to do so. After a while, my lack of backing up skills became well known, and the customer's rig hands would compete to be the first to reach me so that they could get paid to back up my trailer.

When I say we started with a humble shop, that might be stretching a little. It wasn't that impressive. Our first location was a Quonset hut-style of building that was open on the ends and didn't even have lights. When we needed to work at night, we parked vehicles at each end and turned on their headlights. But at least it had a roof. I didn't realize at the time how important that was. For a short period of time we moved out of that building and worked out of a friend's location. They had a large yard and we used a portion of their space. While there, we had to work in the open. That meant working outside in the rain, as well as during sandstorms, cold nights, and hot days, and doing so without any lights beyond our headlights. Eventually, we got into another building. This building wasn't much, but at least we now had an enclosed shop with lights and locking doors.

The new shop was a big improvement, but it didn't have an office. I had a small office in Midland that I had been using for personal business prior to opening Wildcat Oil Tools. My sister and I continued to use it for Wildcat Oil Tools business, but for each of our employees, their office, by and large, was their vehicle. Everyone carried pre-printed invoices in their trucks, and most people did their paperwork in the field. Some people, unfortunately, had the same problems that I did writing hard enough or clearly enough

CHAPTER 4

on invoices and my sister spent a lot of time on the phone chasing people down trying to figure out what they had written.

We got through one day at a time and one problem at a time. Looking back, this was when our winning Mindset began to take shape. It would have been easy to get discouraged and quit, but we hung in there and persevered. Everyone firmly believed the day's problem would be solved and that things would improve. Problems were solved and things did improve.

In the early days, the keyword was "improvise." For example, because we didn't have an office, we scheduled meetings elsewhere. For sales calls, it was easy. Our salesmen and I met with customers and potential customers at their office or work site. If that wasn't viable, we frequently met with people at restaurants. Whatever it took, we did it. We all knew eventually Wildcat Oil Tools would have nice offices, support personnel, and top-flight technology, but right then we had what we had. Nonetheless, somehow, someway, we always managed to get things done because everyone had a "can-do" attitude. People didn't spend time complaining about what we didn't have; instead, they focused on finding a solution to the current problem with the resources that we did have.

For example, when a customer returned a BOP, it had to be cleaned and serviced. Today we have nice shops with cranes, wash bays, and paint bays for jobs like this. In the beginning, we didn't have any that. We cleaned our BOPs at self-service carwashes at night. (You get some interesting looks when you do that.) The service process for BOPs includes repainting them. Since we didn't have a paint bay, we painted the BOPs on the back of trucks or on trailers. And because I only had four BOPs and I had to keep all four of them out earning income as much as possible, cleaning and servicing was frequently done late at night to make sure that a BOP could go back into service for another customer early the next morning.

The one thing that I could do as well as the best of my competition was to develop personal relationships with our customers. I spent time with them on location and I got to know them personally. I also gained their trust because my BOPs were well-maintained, and I kept my promises. That trustworthiness led to an unanticipated development. Customers started asking if I had other pieces of equipment. The first time or two this happened, I probably muddled the response. With practice, I learned to ask, "When do you need it?" Followed by "Let me see."

When I started adding equipment, I kept a handwritten list of our inventory on a single piece of paper. I knew every piece of equipment on that list and I knew I didn't have what the customer was asking for; but I didn't want to admit that without first trying to figure something out. This tactic gave me some time to see if I could find a solution.

I would then call a buddy, Johnny Boy. Sometimes our conversation started "Hey, Johnny Boy, what's an X?" because I didn't even know for sure what the piece of equipment was for which the customer was looking. I'd then find out where I could get one, how much it cost, and what he thought I could rent it for. I learned early in this process several other key questions to ask the customer—such as, "What size and what type of thread?"—during that first call to avoid having to make follow-up calls.

If I could purchase the equipment that the customer wanted, and I was confident that I could rent it often enough to make a profit, I'd

CHAPTER 4

buy it, paint it blue, and would put my serial number on it. I'd then add that piece of equipment and its rental price to my handwritten equipment list. As that list expanded, our new inventory became a point of pride.

In the beginning, I was obviously not an expert on rental tools, but my prior service company experience allowed me to overcome this. In the service business, you're either your customer's problem-solver, or you'll soon be looking for another career. I had plenty of experience identifying a customer's problem and working with others within the company to find a solution that we could offer, so I had more confidence than I probably should have had. Fortunately, more often than not, I was able to get what the customer needed and get it to them when they needed it. However, I never made a commitment that I couldn't deliver. It's always difficult to turn an order down and it was definitely difficult at the beginning because I needed the business. However, I'd rather have someone disappointed in me for turning down an order that I couldn't fill than to be angry at me later for failing to keep a promise. As a result, my customers' confidence in Wildcat Oil Tools increased, our inventory of rental equipment expanded, and repeat business grew.

Some equipment, like BOPs, we deliver to the well site when the customer needs it and we retrieve it when they're finished with it. Other equipment, such as pumps, is rented with an operator. The customer tells us what type of pump they need, when they need it, and where to put it when it's delivered to their location. When it's time to begin using the pump, our employee operates it. When my list of equipment started including operator-run tools, I had to hire operators both because of my lack of experience and because of my other commitments. I was careful to hire good people and to not overstaff. I didn't hire an operator unless I was confident that I had enough work to keep them occupied. I also put off hiring administrative employees as long as possible because they didn't earn me any direct income, but they did increase my overhead.

During this process, my Vision began to take shape. I had backed into the tool rental business to recoup an investment. However, my pride in that growing, handwritten product list eventually morphed into a Vision: to make Wildcat Oil Tools the premier fishing and tool rental company in the world. Looking back, that Vision was almost comical at the time. We had a single and humble location, minimal equipment, and a handful of people. Wildcat Oil Tools, the company, had a limited history and wasn't known outside the Midland-Odessa area. How could I realistically expect to turn that into a nationwide company, let alone a company that could successfully compete with well-established, publicly-traded companies internationally? The answer is that first, I had a Plan: I would recruit world-class talent and we would operate Wildcat Oil Tools from day one as if we already were an international, top-flight service company. And second, I surrounded myself with people who were driven to succeed.

When I started recruiting, I looked for people who fit my Vision. In other words, I wanted the type of people that you'd expect to see at the best fishing and rental tool company in the world. When I found someone that I wanted, I told them about my Vision, described my Plan, and then told them how they fit into that Plan. I found out quickly that the people I wanted invariably found the prospect of being a part of Wildcat Oil Tools' Vision compelling and many

CHAPTER 4

wanted to join. I also quickly learned that people who weren't excited about our Vision weren't good fits.

I didn't realize it at the time, but this is how I found people with the right Mindset. If someone was excited about building a world-class company and believed it was possible, they would naturally persevere through the inevitable challenges to make this Vision a reality. Their Mindset, individually and collectively, became a self-fulfilling prophecy. They saw themselves as part of a world-class company. Therefore, the challenge of the day was simply that, a temporary challenge that could and would be overcome. Because failure wasn't an option, the only question in their minds was how this challenge would be solved. On the other hand, if they weren't excited about our Vision, it was pointless to expect them to be committed to it because they didn't see it happening and, therefore, they were likely to see a challenge as a roadblock.

Our recruiting was also successful because I tried to put myself in the shoes of the people that I was looking for and I asked myself: if I was them, what would I want? Obviously good pay is important, but we've had numerous people take pay cuts to come to work for Wildcat Oil Tools. From talking to people, I learned that from entry-level employees to senior managers, everyone wanted to be treated with respect, they wanted to feel as though they were a valued part of the organization and not simply being used by it, and they wanted a high-quality working environment.

For example, when I recruited Terry Babcock, I noticed he was driving an older pickup, his uniform was unimpressive, and his salary didn't reflect the revenue that he was producing for his employer. Terry is a fisherman. In the oil business, a "fish" is something that is in the wellbore, but shouldn't be, such as a broken drill bit. Fishing is the process of getting the fish out of the wellbore. A fisherman is the individual who does the fishing. Fishermen are highly trained, and they use specialized tools and equipment. Fishing tools and equipment are as critical to their success as surgical instruments are to a surgeon.

Terry mentioned to me that he had to use old tools and equipment and that he didn't appreciate it because the tools made his job more difficult and they reflected on him. Imagine that you've hired someone to do repair work at your house or business. If they walk in looking like a pro, you assume that they are, but if they walk in and their equipment is in poor shape, you naturally assume that they aren't well qualified. Terry didn't appreciate being judged by the appearance of his equipment, the increased difficulty that caused in his job, or the income it cost him.

To understand Terry's frustration, it is important to appreciate his working conditions. Oil and gas wells are drilled and maintained twenty-four-seven, 365 days a year. Today's horizontal wells cost millions of dollars to drill and the longer it takes to drill and complete one, the more it costs the oil company. After a well comes online and begins producing, any equipment failure normally means the well must be shut-in and, therefore, it produces no revenue until it is repaired and returned to service. Consequently, in the oil patch, time truly is money. If an oil company encounters a problem while drilling a well or it has mechanical issues with a producing well, and they need a fisherman to fix the problem; they want one now and they want the fish recovered and the well or wellbore returned to service yesterday. When a fisherman arrives on location, they frequently stay there until the job is finished, which often means working on a job site for twelve to fourteen hours—or more—at a time. Fishermen are outside all night in the middle of the winter and all day in the middle of the summer. Because of the stakes, their work can be stressful. Consequently, if a fisherman is unhappy with his working conditions, he has plenty of time and opportunity for this unhappiness to fester and grow.

Operators, the people who go out with equipment such as pumps, faced similar issues. Most operators receive a base salary and earn bonus money when they are out in the field working on a job. This bonus is like the commission that a sales representative earns on their sales. If you're an operator responsible for a pump or reverse unit, and your equipment breaks down in the field, you can't earn any bonus money until your equipment is repaired or replaced. Bonus money is a significant portion of an operator's income. Many earn more bonus money than they receive in base salary. If an operator has been given older equipment that hasn't been properly maintained, and they feel powerless to prevent or at least minimize downtime for equipment failure, it causes significant frustration and anxiety.

I told Terry about my Vision and that I expected to accomplish it in ten years. Terry was skeptical. He asked me how old I was and how did—he implied—a kid like me, intend to create an international service company? I described my Plan. Thankfully, he believed me because he was a significant reason we not only survived but prospered from the beginning. He attracted both customers and other fishermen. This business and talent were the oxygen that we needed to take off.

When Terry joined Wildcat Oil Tools, I gave him a new pickup and new tools. At that time, none of our competitors were giving their fisherman new vehicles or fishing equipment. Everyone else required their fishermen to make do with older vehicles and equipment. Obviously, you have to control your costs and I can understand why a company would try to get away with older vehicles and equipment for its fishermen and operators. However, when you're asking someone who is generating a lot of revenue for you, to work twelve to fourteen hours at a time outside in stressful and difficult conditions, you can't ignore their working conditions—at least not if you want to keep them. I was intent on making our fisherman and operators happy both to encourage greater productivity and to lower turnover.

I followed a similar process for our other employees. In each case I tried to put myself in their shoes and then asked myself if I were them what would I want and need to be happy, productive, and successful. For our fishermen and operators, new trucks and tools, as well as well-maintained rental equipment, were big-ticket items; but frequently it was little things that mattered. For example, they appreciated good-looking, comfortable uniforms, being treated with respect, and having access to someone who was willing to listen to them. That cost me little to nothing but when I provided it, my people realized that I cared about them, and they usually reciprocated. For example, they praised Wildcat Oil Tools to their friends and if they got a job offer from a competitor, they turned it down even though they would have received a raise. The word-of-mouth publicity this generated was priceless.

CHAPTER 4

Another key to our early growth was that even though we were a small company, we never acted like it. We made every effort to look and act like a professional, world-class company. We equipped our people with the same tools and equipment that a world-class company would use, and we followed the same job processes that a world-class company would have. When I say job processes, I'm referring to formalized, standard operating procedures (SOPs). We had written processes in place for the services that we performed and for our equipment's maintenance. These processes promoted safe, consistent work practices, which in turn led to more work as our track record for working safely and getting the done job correctly became more well known.

One way to visualize the effect of our job processes is to consider a nationally-franchised restaurant versus a locally-owned restaurant. When you walk into McDonald's and order your favorite hamburger, even if it's the first time that you've been to this particular location, you expect it to look and taste exactly the same as every other McDonald's hamburger that you've ever ordered. When you go to a locally-owned restaurant for the first time, you're uncertain what to expect. This uncertainty sometimes leads us to choose a nationally-franchised restaurant over a locally-owned one.

Fear of the unknown is a concept that is definitely present in the oil and gas industry. When you're drilling a hole one to two miles straight down and then laterally one to two more miles through solid rock, positioning pipe and cement in the hole while only having contact with it at the surface, making small holes in the pipe and cement at predetermined locations miles away from your drilling rig, and then creating small fractures in the rock immediately outside the small holes, several things can go wrong. Oil and gas companies are consistently looking for ways to minimize their risk. One way to do so is by eliminating any uncertainty over what to expect from a service company. Wildcat's job processes promoted consistency. Thus, our customers knew what to expect when they hired us for a job and this certainty lead to trust and more work.

Somewhere along the line, a funny thing happened. Even though we were a small, start-up company, our people looked, acted, and performed as if they were part of a world-class company. They say that perception is reality. If you look and act the part long enough, your customers will eventually believe it too. This perception, along with our safety and success track record, got us work with companies that wouldn't ordinarily hire a small service company.

Our initial growth also benefitted from the fact that the oilfield fishing community is comparatively small. Terry was well respected by his peers and fishermen like to compare notes. When Terry came to work for Wildcat Oil Tools, people heard he'd started working for a company about which many knew nothing. They then saw, or heard from others, that Terry was driving a new truck and that he was using new tools and equipment. That information sparked interest. People started talking to Terry to find out what was going on and who the heck was Wildcat Oil Tools. Terry was a great recruiter. Within weeks, I started receiving calls from other experienced fishermen who wanted to come to work for Wildcat Oil Tools if they could also get a new truck and equipment.

We had all the usual problems that start-up companies encounter. I was willing to work with our people to find creative solutions, but I never compromised on my strategic Plan. Wildcat

CHAPTER 4

Oil Tools always looked, acted, and operated as if we were an industry-leading, international service company. There were times when my commitment was tested and several of those are set out in this book; but because the people whom I recruited fit my image, they came to Wildcat Oil Tools expecting to work for a world-class service company, and they were treated accordingly, I always had considerable buy-in and support from my employees.

Employee buy-in and support are critical for all the obvious reasons. They were particularly important to Wildcat Oil Tools because our credibility depended on it. As I've noted, today's horizontal wells cost millions to drill. No oil company will risk this investment by using vendors they don't trust. The experienced fishermen and operators who joined Wildcat Oil Tools gave us some instant credibility because our customers knew them. Wildcat's credibility was enhanced when our fishermen and operators arrived on location with well-maintained equipment and good-looking trucks and uniforms. Wildcat's credibility was bolstered even further when every one of our fishermen and operators followed the same industry-leading processes and procedures. We were able to do that only because our managers and employees bought into the Wildcat Oil Tools Vision.

Terry not only recruited talent and customers, he's the reason why our colors became black and yellow. My first BOPs were blue when they were purchased. When we cleaned and dressed them, I continued painting them blue. I also painted the other tools that I had added to our list of products blue. One day Terry came by the barn we called a shop and said, "A lot of the competition is blue, so we should paint our tools and pumps black." He pointed out that black tools would set us apart and that black trucks "would look awesome." I thought about it and agreed. We then repainted everything black. Fortunately, we didn't have a lot of inventory at the time, so the pain was minimal. From that point on, all our tools and equipment have been painted black with yellow trim.

The color story is significant for two reasons. First, it was critical to our branding, which I'll discuss further in a later chapter. Second, it confirmed to Terry that he was a member of a team. As I noted earlier, I quickly learned our potential employees were so interested in being treated with respect and as team members, that they'd take a pay cut to come work for Wildcat Oil Tools and would turn down a pay raise to stay with us. To make them feel like a team member, I knew that it was important that I not only listen to my people, I knew I had to seek their feedback and to empower them to become engaged in the process of fulfilling my Vision.

Buy-in and empowerment are buzzwords that most companies use but not all companies achieve. It's a shame because I can't imagine how you ever obtain a committed workforce without it. When your people don't feel like they're a part of a team, you wind up with compliant employees. There is a critical difference between compliance and commitment. A compliant employee shows up for work when required, works till their shift ends, and does everything required of them by the job—but rarely anything else. A committed employee takes the extra step without being asked and encourages their co-workers to do likewise.

You can't be everywhere, hear everything, or know everything. Collectively, your employees do. If they are committed to your Vision, they'll do or suggest things that you'd never considered,

CHAPTER 4

will solve problems before you hear about them, and will do the little extra things for a customer that makes all the difference in the world. They'll do these things because they've taken ownership of the Vision. An organization full of people who've taken ownership of a Vision is a powerful force.

CHAPTER FIVE

MINDSET

As I've previously noted, when I started writing this book, I came to realize how important the right Mindset was to our success. Before I continue with Wildcat Oil Tools' story, I'm going to focus on Mindset, and I'll explain how it works and why it's so important for you individually and for your organization. I'll also show you how you can create the right Mindset both for yourself and your organization.

Your mind is the single most important tool that you possess. It can empower you to achieve the amazing or lock you into mediocrity. Remember the story of the Little Engine that Could? A train full of toys is being sent to a town on the other side of the mountain for Christmas. The train breaks down at the base of the mountain and a clown tries to get another engine to pull the train over the mountain. Several engines refuse for a variety of suspicious-sounding reasons. Then a small engine, apparently incapable of pulling the train up the mountain, offers to help. It hooks up to the train and starts pulling the toys. When the grade becomes steep and the engine starts to struggle, it begins saying, "I think I can! I think I can!" and continues plugging up the mountain. Eventually the little engine makes it to the top of the mountain and the toys are delivered to the children in time for Christmas. The moral of the story is that the little train's courage and self-confidence allowed it to succeed when the other engines wouldn't even try.

I can't promise you that the right Mindset will guarantee success—but I can guarantee you that the wrong Mindset will produce failure and I promise you that the right Mindset will maximize your chances of reaching your Vision. The good news is that unlike attributes such as height or looks, you have control over your Mindset. You want to improve it? I'll show you how. The bad news is that even a single person can negatively impact your organization's Mindset. I'll show you what to look for so that this doesn't happen to you.

When you think Mindset, people often think of confidence. There is no doubt that confidence is critically important, but it's just one of several keys to the right Mindset. You also have to be relentless in the pursuit of your dream; you must be willing to learn continually—especially from failure. You can't allow wishful thinking to substitute for hard work or anything else; and you must always be cognizant of your team and its needs.

The importance of being relentless is self-evident. I doubt anyone starts off believing there will be no setbacks, but I'm not sure everyone truly understands and appreciates what being relentless entails when you start a new business or venture. For one, the start-up process requires sustained perseverance and determination. It's easy to start strong, but the key is continuing when you're physically and emotionally worn out, when you've taken several body blows, or when you're struggling with a difficult problem that has no obvious solution.

You often see a success story that appears to have happened overnight or as the result of a single big break. In my experience, there's no such thing as overnight success. I'll bet that if you take a hard look at an overnight success, you'll find out that the successful person or group put in a substantial amount of time and effort and overcame several setbacks and disappointments before getting their big break and that without this previous effort and refusal to accept defeat, there would have been no big break.

I seriously doubt many people accomplish their Vision without the journey taking unexpected turns and detours. At Wildcat Oil Tools, we focus a lot of time and effort on planning and we've profited mightily from it, but rare was the time when events played out as we hoped. Far more often, accomplishing a project took longer, involved more effort, and cost more than we had anticipated because of unexpected negative developments. But because we were always relentless in our pursuit of the Wildcat Oil Tools Vision, unexpected bad news didn't deter us.

One way that we overcame setbacks was through continual repetition of our Vision. In fact, we never described Wildcat's future any other way. You can do the same for yourself. When an unexpected problem hits, stay positive. Even if you don't know how you're going to solve it, repeatedly tell yourself that you can and will accomplish your Vision. Stay positive. Be your own version of the little engine that could.

Reminding yourself to stay positive is important because when unexpected problems hit, a little voice in your head frequently starts expressing doubt and, if left unchecked, it'll fill your head with negativity. Unfortunately, you can't simply tell yourself never to have a negative thought, or, when one occurs, to tell yourself to stop thinking negatively. If you try that, you'll probably find that the harder you tell yourself not to think negatively, the more likely you are to think of little else. Instead, when that voice starts to sow doubt, replace the negative thought with a positive one.

Imagine you're a golfer facing a difficult tee shot over a pond. If you set up over the ball telling yourself, "Don't hit it into the water! Don't hit it into the water!" odds are pretty high that unless you hit your shot so poorly it doesn't reach the water, it's going to get wet. On the other hand, the golfer who sets up over the ball telling themselves, "You've got this, you're hitting the ball well today, put it on the back ledge," has a much higher chance of success because they're planning for success rather than trying to avoid failure.

You can do this in business too. Imagine you've been hit with a significant and unexpected problem such as a customer, vendor, or employment issue. It's perfectly natural for you to feel anxious, since the problem was unexpected. That anxiety, however, is what's feeding the negative voice in your head. Fortunately, when you realize what's giving fuel to the doubt, it's that much easier to stop it. Take a deep breath and say to yourself, "We've got this; we've solved far worse problems than this," and then start thinking about the steps that you'll take to identify, address, or solve the problem. You can't think about two things at once. If you start thinking about the things you're going to do to solve the problem, that automatically means you're not entertaining any self-doubt.

CHAPTER 5

Positive thinking is not only a tool to handle anxiety, it's good for you in general too. Think of it as a form of food for your mind. Your body reflects the food you eat; so, too, your Mindset reflects what you feed your mind. Just as you should avoid smoking and unhealthy food, you can't let the little voice in your head run amok when you're facing a challenge. It's also another reason why it's so important to associate yourself with the right people. If you surround yourself with people who continually tell you that you can't do something, sooner or later you'll start to believe that yourself and you won't even try to achieve something spectacular. This is one of the reasons why I didn't hire or keep people who couldn't see Wildcat Oil Tools becoming a first-class international service company.

Associating yourself with positive people is no less important in your personal life. Imagine a young man or woman being raised by parents who continually tell them they're stupid, slow, lazy, and will never amount to anything. How likely is it that this young man or woman will live up to their potential? My guess is that sooner or later they will begin to live down to the negative comments and will become the individual that their parents are describing. What if the same young man or woman was raised by parents who continually reinforced the notion that their child had unlimited potential and with hard work could become anything they wanted? I'd be willing to bet on them. Positive feedback doesn't ensure a child will become the next president of the US, or that an employee will meet your expectations, but it definitely improves their chances.

Negative people don't just impact your sense of self-worth, they steal energy. Have you ever spent time with someone who constantly complained and criticized? I have. A few minutes with them wears me out. You could give them a golden brick and they'd complain that it was too heavy. Don't get me wrong, I want my friends to come to me when they've got a problem that I can help with. What I'm talking about is the person who never has a positive comment about anyone or anything, who continually burdens others with their problems, and who is a drama king or queen. When you start to take on their problems, it's hard not to get down.

On the other hand, consider the person who is so positive and so full of energy that every time you're with them you find yourself smiling and feeling more optimistic about life in general. Suddenly, the sun's a little brighter, your problems are more manageable, and your ability to handle the day's challenges improves—all of that because a little of their positive energy rubbed off on you. You can't always choose who you work with, but you can choose who you associate yourself with after work. Do whatever it takes to avoid the Debbie and David Downers, the gossips, and the people who continually pour water on your dreams. If you can't avoid them at work, at least minimize their impact on you.

Negative people can ruin an organization's Mindset. Their constant criticism and gossip act like a cancer. Nothing you do will ever make them happy for long and, in fact, if you try to respond to one of their criticisms to make them happy, you only empower them to criticize more. In my experience, at best they lower morale and at worst their bad attitude spreads. That's why I'm always careful when I encounter someone at Wildcat Oil Tools who is always negative, and if they can't change their behavior, we make a personnel change.

Obviously, you can take this principle too far if you refuse to hear or consider any negative comment or if your people become

CHAPTER 5

afraid to raise questions or concerns. Healthy mental input, just like your diet, requires balance. Green vegetables are good for you but eating nothing else probably isn't. If you can't distinguish between a negative person and a team member with a constructive comment, you'll find yourself surrounded by yes-men and women and you'll hear nothing but positive feedback—right up until the moment your organization fails.

Encouraging balance is critical. I don't know of anyone who doesn't have a bad idea occasionally. Lord knows that I've had a few. If I'm considering doing something stupid, I need to know it. My goal as CEO is to create an environment where people aren't afraid to speak up when they see a problem or potential mistake. This doesn't mean they aren't committed to your Vision, far from it; but it means they're committed to making the Vision a reality. I'm totally committed to the Wildcat Oil Tools Vision and I have no interest in compromising that Vision; I am, however, willing to consider different options for achieving it.

So, how do you tell the difference between a good team member who is willing to challenge a questionable decision from a negative person who criticizes simply because that's what they do? To me, one difference between the two is intent. I have no idea what motivates a negative person. I've always been an optimist and I can't fathom any other way of thinking. If you truly believe you're surrounded by idiots and that the company is being run into the ground, how can you get out of bed in the morning? Because of this, I have no idea what a negative person's intent is other than to make everyone else feel bad. But a good team member with a criticism is motivated to see us succeed. For Wildcat Oil Tools, that has always been an individual who believed in our Vision and wanted to make it happen, but who was concerned that something we were doing or were considering doing wouldn't help us accomplish our dream. Frequently, you'll see this person follow up a criticism with a suggestion. That type of behavior is not only fine with me, it's something I want to cultivate at Wildcat Oil Tools. As long as we're aligned on the goal, I have no problem with someone looking for better ways to succeed. It's the person who doesn't believe in the Vision that I want to separate myself from.

Another difference between the two is their response to being told "no." No one gets their way 100 percent of the time. If you're currently a CEO, I'm sure you've had situations where an investor, bank, customer, or your Board of Directors overruled you, or, alternatively, your senior team members opposed something so strenuously that you eventually gave in. If you're not yet the CEO, I'm equally sure you've had times when your boss said "no" to one of your ideas or suggestions. The point is that for every one of us, there are times when the organization's decision isn't the one that we individually would make. What your people do after being told "no" is critical to your organization's Mindset.

A good team member puts aside their personal disappointment and supports the organization's decision. A negative person complains and uses this decision as another example of why they're the smartest person in the room and the organization is being run by idiots. The negative person will even try to sabotage the decision through their lack of support, if not outright opposition. The team member works as hard to make the organization's decision successful as they would if it were their own idea. If a person can't support

CHAPTER 5

Wildcat Oil Tools unless they get their way, they aren't going to stay long if I have anything to say about it.

Let's get back to your personal Mindset. To achieve your full potential, you must think big and act big. I mean really big. Not something that when you achieve it, people will say "good for you" or "that's nice." You want something that will cause others to blurt out, "Oh wow!" When you've got that big Vision and you're 100 percent committed to it, vividly picture yourself successfully achieving it. What will that look like? What will people say? How will you react? Work on those images until they are as clear in your head as if you were looking at pictures taken on a high-quality camera.

This visualization is critical because our thoughts are powerful. In fact, our thoughts are so powerful that they're self-defining. The person who tells themselves they probably aren't good enough isn't. The person who dwells on problems attracts others. However, the person who remains optimistic finds solutions and opportunities. The person who tells themselves they can do it, often does. Seeing your Vision come true is not only the best way that I know of to convince yourself that it can and will happen, but you'll find yourself automatically doing the things that must be done to make that Vision come true.

This self-generated belief is crucial to your success. Too often we limit ourselves by not truly believing we can achieve a goal until we actually do so. Until then, we give ourselves an excuse to come up short by saying, "I'll do my best." If we later come up short, we say, "I wasn't successful, but I did my best." If that's in fact true, so be it—but did you really do your best? Keep in mind that your best isn't measured by what you're capable of doing today but by what you're capable of achieving tomorrow. The person who justifies their failure by saying, "I did my best," is unknowingly saying they aren't worthy because if their best wasn't good enough to accomplish something, then their potential is limited. Don't give yourself an easy out. Instead, give yourself a real challenge, tell everyone what it is, and then get after it with no thought of anything except success.

Obviously, it's easy to say you're going to stay positive, but when you attempt the spectacular, harboring some doubts or struggling with some fear of failure is human nature. For many, the fear of failure is actually a powerful motivator. If that motivation works for you, great, but don't let the anxiety limit you. Be your own cheerleader throughout the process. Repeatedly tell yourself that you're going to pull this off. Celebrate every intermediate success. Keep working on that mental picture of your ultimate success. It takes practice and concentrated effort at first, but the day that you realize how powerful your thoughts are, is the day you'll stop allowing yourself to dwell on the negative ones.

One way to deal with the anxiety is by consciously growing personally. Expand your boundaries by continuing to learn. There is no limit to what you can learn. Challenge yourself to learn a new language or to play a new musical instrument or to read a book every month. When you accomplish your challenge, find a new one. I can't think of a better way to foster self-confidence than by setting and achieving personal goals. Do the same for your team by continually encouraging its members to challenge themselves. Give someone a measurable goal such as improving sales or cutting costs by X percent or create some friendly competition between two offices or groups. Monitor their performance and reward success.

CHAPTER 5

You may have noticed I said to reward success and I didn't encourage you to give everyone a participation trophy. I hate participation trophies because they deemphasize the importance of winning. I understand that well-meaning people want to soften the blow for those who didn't win; but because there are no participation trophies in life, we shouldn't shield our kids from the consequences of failing.

You can't shield yourself from failure. In fact, when you try to do something spectacular, you run the risk of failing spectacularly. Failing stinks. It hurts and it can be embarrassing. Really embarrassing. And guess what, it should. You never want to reach a point where failure becomes even close to acceptable. So then why should you increase the risk of failing dramatically by thinking and acting big? Why not set a smaller goal with the intent of building on initial success? First, you'll never realize your full potential unless your Vision borders on the outlandish, for only then are you putting yourself in a position where you absolutely have to grow and give it your all. Second, thinking big and having incremental successes aren't mutually inconsistent. If you're Vision truly is big, you're going to have to grow to achieve it and you will necessarily cross several milestones in the process.

The fact that you might fail is no reason to avoid the risk. Even if things go horribly wrong, you're a better person for having made the effort. In 1910, Teddy Roosevelt gave what has become known as "The Man in the Arena" speech. In it he said:

> It is not the critic who counts. Not the man who points out how the strong man stumbles or where the doer of deeds could have done them better. The

> credit belongs to the man who is actually in the arena, whose face is marred by dust and sweat and blood, who strives valiantly, who errs, who comes up short again and again, because there is no effort without error and shortcoming; but who does actually strive to do the deeds, who knows great enthusiasms, the great devotions, who spends himself in a worthy cause, who at best knows in the end the triumph of high achievement, and who at the worst, if he fails, at least fails while daring greatly, so that his place shall never be with those cold and timid souls who neither know victory nor defeat.

Don't be the person who never experiences victory or defeat; rather, dare to be the one with the courage to step into the arena.

So why am I spending time talking about failure when this is supposed to be about having a winning Mindset? Simple. Quite often, what feels like a failure is, in fact, just a setback. Setbacks can be overcome. If you didn't achieve your Vision but have an opportunity to try it again or to try something similar, you didn't fail, you've just had a setback. In the beginning of this book I shared the story of Henry Ford. When we think of him today, we think of his tremendous successes with the Ford Motor Company. We often forget that this was his third company. The first two went broke. Walt Disney filed for bankruptcy when his first company failed. Milton Hershey, the founder of Hershey's Chocolate, filed for bankruptcy twice. When their companies closed, I'm sure it felt like a failure. Lord knows I would be devastated if Wildcat Oil Tools went under. Looking back, however, it's clear to us that Henry Ford, Walt Disney, and Milton

CHAPTER 5

Hershey weren't failures. They had temporary setbacks which they overcame through hard work, dedication, and persistence.

If you remember nothing else from this chapter, I want you to keep in mind two things. First, like Yogi Berra said, "It isn't over till it's over." As long as you're still plugging, your Vision is alive and well. Second, not only should you be willing to learn from mistakes and setbacks, you should consciously do so. At Wildcat Oil Tools, we worked hard to develop a culture where failure wasn't an option, but setbacks were expected. When the inevitable setback occurred, I didn't want people panicking, nor did I want anyone to be afraid to own up to a mistake. Instead, I wanted people to have the self-confidence in Wildcat Oil Tools to see us finding a solution and the personal self-confidence to learn from their mistakes. To accomplish this transformation, I had to encourage people to think positively, not defensively. That meant that I needed them to own up to problems and that I set the right example.

You set the right example initially by what you do when you first get bad news. My advice is to do nothing until you're sure that the immediate emotion has passed and that you're back in control. That cooling-down period will prevent you from shooting the messenger—which is important if you want your team to be honest with you. It'll also help you avoid overreacting. Recognize that your emotions can cause you to overstate a problem. With reflection, you'll frequently find the problem isn't as bad as it first appeared. That insight promotes taking a measured approach and, in the process, will help you avoid making the problem worse.

When you do react, take the high road. I've gotten angry and said some things that I soon regretted; but I've rarely regretted the things that I didn't say when I was upset. I haven't solved a lot of problems when I was negative. When I'm negative, it tends to make the remainder of my team negative or anxious. That attitude doesn't promote solutions. That doesn't mean I don't hold people accountable—I do and if you want to be successful, you should too. But I don't allow myself to go off on a tirade in front of others.

As quickly as you can, shift gears. Put things in perspective. What exactly has happened? Strip away the emotions and other baggage and get to the facts. A certain amount of venting is normal, but I've never seen a problem solved with bitching or bellyaching. Force yourself and your group to focus on solutions and alternatives. The quicker you can achieve this focus, the quicker that you'll solve the problem.

Learn from mistakes. Find out what specifically went wrong. Why? How do we avoid repeating this mistake? As you're doing this, never let your ego—or anyone else's—prevent the organization from determining that there's a better way to do things. For Wildcat Oil Tools, this meant periodically adjusting our approach. There were times when an attempt to land a new customer or to expand with a new product didn't work. When we took a critical look, we sometimes realized things didn't work because we had made a mistake. When that happened, we didn't give up; instead, we looked for a new opportunity and we developed a strategy that incorporated the lessons we had learned.

Disappointment can be a highly effective learning tool if you'll set aside your ego and take a critical look at yourself. Self-scrutiny is painful, but it's definitely effective. When something that I was involved in doesn't work, it's frequently hard to admit that at least part of the problem is my fault. Instead, I'm tempted to lash out at others. If you allow yourself to engage in this type of behavior, your people will be afraid to admit they made a mistake for fear of getting embarrassed or fired. You can't let your ego prevent you or others from engaging in critical analysis. Notice I said "let." I say that because even if you don't have control over the emotion you experience when you first hear bad news, you have complete control over what you do in response. Your action today will shape your team's response to future bad news and, more importantly, your pattern of behavior will become your team's pattern of behavior when the inevitable setbacks occur.

I believed in our strategies and investments and I could have easily refused to acknowledge that I had made a mistake and continued trying to do the same thing the same way. In that case, I would have wasted more capital on bad investments and more time on bad strategies. If you set the example by owning up to your mistakes, you make it easier for others to do the same. You can foster that response if you make clear that you're looking for solutions, not scapegoats.

Throughout this chapter, I've focused almost exclusively on improving your Mindset through positive thinking and similar steps. I did so because it works. However, never allow wishful thinking to substitute for action. Earlier I described my Polo boots. I could have spent a lot of time wishing that I had a pair and, had I done so, I would have never gotten them. Instead, I put them on layaway and I went out and mowed lawns until I had enough money to pay them off. The same holds true for your Vision. Visualizing success is critical to achieving a Vision, but it's a start, not a Plan. As soon as you've got your Vision, incorporate a Plan, and then act on it publicly. Your Plan won't be a work of art, and it doesn't even have to be complete.

It's also okay if your first step is a misstep because simply taking the first step is huge.

Admiral William McRaven gave perhaps the most popular commencement address ever at the University of Texas in 2014. It became known as the "Make Your Bed" speech. Admiral McRaven was a Navy SEAL for over thirty years and he took the lessons that he had learned while becoming a SEAL to illustrate how the new graduates could change the world. The first was to make their bed every day. He noted it was a small, mundane action, but he pointed out that accomplishing the first task of the day leads to a small sense of pride and it encourages a person to accomplish the next task, which in turn encourages them to accomplish yet another task, and so forth.

I agree with Admiral McRaven wholeheartedly. When you've developed a Vision, daily positive action is critically important. In the beginning, action is transformational. We all wish for things, and while a certain amount of daydreaming is probably healthy, it's never a recipe for success. When you take that first public step to implement your Vision, you transform it from "I want" or "I'd like" to "I'm doing." When I saw that pair of Polo boots in the mall, they were something that I wanted. When I put them on layaway and started mowing lawns, they became something that I was earning.

Action is also important because success breeds success. Just like making your bed in the morning provides a small sense of pride, when I got the first lawn-mowing job, it gave me the confidence to continue asking for work. At Wildcat Oil Tools, when I got our first MSA, it gave me the confidence to pursue other contracts. When we added product lines and were able to keep that equipment rented, it gave us the confidence to add additional product lines. Similarly, when we successfully expanded to New Mexico, it gave us the confidence to continue expanding.

It's fun to look back on the days where we achieved something big, but daily small steps have outsized consequence. Start every day with a positive step forward. Personally, I like to work out first thing in the morning. Besides the physical benefits of working out, the sense of accomplishment fuels my self-confidence. When I get to the office, making sure my desk is clean is another small step with real benefit because it gives me a feeling of control. Find a day-starting event that works for you. Perhaps it's working out, reading your unopened email, or making your bed. The actual event isn't as important as finding something that you can do every day and then making sure that you do it. You'll find that giving yourself a feeling of control and success will pay off handsomely over the course of your career.

A feeling of having some control over your circumstances is unbelievably important. Oftentimes, there are risks to your organization and Vision that you simply cannot control. For Wildcat Oil Tools, one of the risks that we face is that oil and gas prices will drop significantly, and, as a result, our customers will cut back their activities or go out of business. There's nothing that I can do that will have any impact on commodity prices. Thus, there's little point worrying about it; but if I'm not careful, worrying about it is all that I'll do. That's why I've focused most of this discussion on your personal Mindset because you control it and if your Mindset isn't right, your organization's Mindset isn't likely to be right either.

Before I continue, a word of caution: I've spent a lot of time telling you to be your own cheerleader, but don't let your desire to develop the right personal Mindset cause you to become self-absorbed. Be sure to lift up others. It's not only good for them, it's good for you. It's amazing how much you learn when you teach others. My general counsel was in the Army and he tells me that frequently when the Army wanted someone to learn something, they assigned them the task of teaching that topic to their unit. I found that the same holds true in the business world. I've benefitted tremendously from mentors. I try to return the favor by mentoring others. As I've done so, I've been amazed at how much I learned. I've also discovered when I lift up others, I become much sharper myself.

I want to close this chapter on Mindset with a final thought: enjoy the journey! Throughout this book I have emphasized the need to look forward and visualize, to plan, and to exercise discipline if you want to optimize how close you come to achieving your full potential. This is a forward-looking approach that may require some sacrifice, but if your Vision is worthwhile, you'll never regret it. On the other hand, don't focus so exclusively on the goal that you disregard the journey.

There are several keys to enjoying the journey. First, if you don't enjoy the activities necessary to make your Vision a reality, find another Vision. I've spent my entire career in the oil and gas industry because I enjoy it, but this industry isn't for everyone. I've used the example of running a steakhouse to make some of my points because we're all generally familiar with restaurants, but I seriously doubt I'll ever try to run one. I've been involved in a couple of restaurants as an investor. In the process, I've discovered that restaurant operations aren't my passion. If you don't enjoy what you're doing, look for

CHAPTER 5

something that you can be passionate about and find a Vision that complements this passion.

Slow down from time to time to relax. I like to travel and to play golf—at least when I'm playing well. It doesn't matter what your relaxation activity is; the key is to have something that you enjoy doing and something that takes your mind off of your troubles and worries. It takes a lot of energy to worry about things outside your control. If you can refocus your mind on something else, you'll find that you get recharged. I can't think of anything better for a healthy Mindset than a periodic recharge and nothing worse than being worn down by the daily problems.

Get to know the people that you work and associate with. For most of us, the sad reality is that we'll spend more waking hours with our co-workers than with our families. If that's correct, we owe it to ourselves and our co-workers to learn more about each other. Do they have kids? If so, what are their kids involved in? What are their hobbies? Is there something in their lives that they're looking forward to, such as a wedding or a graduation? The more you know about an individual, the easier it is to like them, and the more that you like them the easier it is to work with them. Plus, you'll find yourself enjoying their successes and milestones with them. This camaraderie also helps you maintain a perspective on what's truly important. I spend a lot of time poring over financials and reports. It's important work, but every now and then seeing someone's new baby or grandchild reminds me of what's important and what we as a company are working toward.

CHAPTER SIX

WILDCAT OIL TOOLS' GROWTH, US LOCATIONS

I can look back at our early days with a sense of nostalgia, but at the same time with a great deal of pride in how far we've come. The journey was most definitely an interesting one with lots of stops. I've explained how we added to our product list in the early days by buying equipment in response to customer requests. Had we continued that process, we could have continued to expand the company; however, there would have effectively been a ceiling on our growth, because we were renting the same equipment and providing the same services that numerous other companies were offering. Several things happened that allowed us to grow first into a national company, second into an international company, and third from a boutique service company to a broad-based one with proprietary tools and equipment.

Our first big step was to open a second location in Loving, a small town in southeastern New Mexico. I call this expansion a big step because having a second location required us to double our inventory of equipment and the fact that it was located in another state required us to become more sophisticated administratively. More importantly, the procedures that we followed when we opened the New Mexico location would later become the foundation for our continued expansion.

The fact that we started in the Midland-Odessa area makes sense, because I lived in Midland and this oilfield has always been active, but why Loving, New Mexico? The short answer is that it is an example of following the buffalo herd. I have always stressed the importance of collaborative relationships with our customers. A large part of this collaboration involves encouraging them to tell us how we could do a better job of solving their problems. For example, during one of these conversations, I learned a customer wanted access to larger rental pumps because the pumps he was renting didn't deliver enough pressure for the horizontal wells that his firm was drilling. I did some checking and found out that a larger pump was available and that we could keep it busy, so we added that to our inventory. Not only did adding larger pumps result in additional immediate income, the customer noticed we asked, listened, and responded. Oilfield service companies are in the business of solving problems. We wanted our customers to think of us when they had problems, and this incident encouraged that customer to do so. The incident also gave us favorable word-of-mouth publicity when this company told others what we had done.

In the beginning, our area of operations was necessarily limited because we had a single yard in Odessa, Texas. From our customers, we learned many were becoming more active in southeastern New Mexico and were having problems finding good vendors. More than one customer told us that they'd give us work if we could service

CHAPTER 6

their New Mexico locations. We looked at the geographic area where our current customers were working in New Mexico, the number of wells that were involved, and what it would take to enter a new market. From that we determined that there was enough activity to make a second location profitable. We found a shop building in Loving, New Mexico that we could buy, and then we developed a Plan for financing the purchase of the land and the new equipment that would be needed to open a second shop.

The decision to purchase a shop building rather than lease one was based on our desire to control our own destiny. Renting or leasing a location can be tempting because the upfront cost is less, the landlord may bear some of the repair exposure, and you don't have the risk of being stuck with an unwanted piece of property for the foreseeable future if things don't work out. On the other hand, when you're a tenant, your options are limited to the buildings that are then available to rent. You can have an idea of what the perfect building would look like, where it would be, and how it would be equipped, but unless that building is available to rent now, you have to settle for something else. Moreover, even if you find a building and location that you love, your ability to stay is limited to the term of your lease. When your lease term is over, your future occupancy is subject to the landlord's desires. Finally, even if the landlord wants to continue renting the building to you, rent invariably increases when a new lease is executed, and the new rent may make this location uneconomical.

We decided to buy the Loving location to eliminate the uncertainty of renting and to create a shop and yard that met our Vision. Buying property became our SOP as we continued to expand. There were times when we were forced to rent a location when we first expanded into an area; but even then, we eventually bought property and built our own shop and yard when the right location became available. Looking back with the benefit of twenty-twenty hindsight, I'd do it the same way again, because our facilities were first-rate and their appearance reinforced our Vision of being a world-class company.

Let me get back to our decision to open a second yard in New Mexico. The capital commitment for a second location was a big concern. When you have one-hundred locations and decide to open one more, the required additional inventory is a small percentage of your total assets and, therefore, acquiring one more location isn't a major event; and if the next location doesn't work, you can easily transfer that inventory to one or more of your other locations. When you have only one location, however, adding one more requires you to basically double everything. Doubling our inventory of fishing tools and rental equipment was a major event. If things hadn't worked out in New Mexico, we couldn't have easily absorbed that inventory in our Odessa facility. We would have probably been required to sell a lot of it at a significant loss.

A second location also dramatically increases your administrative obligations. We now had two sets of phone bills and electric bills, double the amount of property to maintain, and new communication challenges. We wanted to handle as much of the administrative work as possible in Midland, so we had to develop a process for completing our New Mexico employees' human resource paperwork in New Mexico but maintaining the records and handling the human resource issues in Midland. Every state has its own set of employment rules, so we had to learn a new set of rules and to develop processes for taking care of Texas and New Mexico payroll under different rules simultaneously. There were also a lot of little challenges. For example, Texas is in the Central Time Zone and New Mexico is in the Mountain. Thus, when we scheduled a conference call, we couldn't say we'll talk at 9:00 a.m., we had to schedule it for 9:00 a.m. Texas time and 8:00 a.m. New Mexico time. Administrative people in Midland had to remember the Loving office opened an hour later, while the people in Loving had to remember the Midland office closed an hour earlier. These are obviously little problems, but I use them to show that a second location forced us to consider and address numerous issues, large and small.

Fortunately, the Loving location was immediately successful. The customers who promised us work came through, and that opened the door to new opportunities because we were exposed to companies that weren't active in west Texas. Consequently, we added some new customers. These new customers frequently resulted in more west Texas work either because of referrals or when they expanded their operations into Texas.

Besides the additional revenue, having a successful second location also benefitted us because it gave us some flexibility with people and equipment. The Loving and Odessa facilities are approximately a two-and-a-half hour drive apart. If you live in a large metropolitan area, that may sound like an extremely long drive, but in west Texas, it's almost next door. For example, Midland and Odessa schools regularly drive their students four-plus hours on school buses for district sporting events, and even farther for pre- and post-season events. Thus, if we needed someone to drive two-and-a-half hours from one facility to the other to drop off or pick up equipment, or to work on a job, no one thought twice about it.

That proximity allowed us to staff the Loving facility with existing employees initially. That overlap simplified things because we didn't have to train anyone on Wildcat's processes and procedures. As you'll recall, I mentioned earlier that we had the same work processes and procedures in place that you'd expect to find at a major service company from the beginning. These processes and procedures promoted safe, consistent, and successful work practices and they helped set us apart from our competitors. Because the people we staffed our New Mexico location with were familiar with our processes and procedures, I didn't have to spend time training a new set of staff or having to worry about inconsistent practices between our Texas and New Mexico locations. The proximity also meant that if one facility needed people or equipment, that facility could frequently borrow what it needed from the other. That proximity saved us some capital and benefitted our fishermen and operators. If one location was short-handed, I could send them help, which allowed our fisherman and operators to stay busy and earn more money.

Our Loving success made the decision to expand again much easier. This time, we decided to expand to Oklahoma. We picked Oklahoma because several of our customers had operations there and they promised us some work, we had some connections to other Oklahoma operators, and it was reasonably close to our current operations. The Oklahoma expansion, however, interjected some additional complexity that helped us with future expansion. When we expanded to Loving, we originally staffed it with current Wildcat Oil Tools employees. We knew that most, if not all, of the Oklahoma employees would be new hires. This necessarily created two problems: first, we had to recruit and hire new people, and then we had to develop a method for instilling and maintaining our culture in a remote location.

When we had one location, it was easy for me to monitor compliance with our job processes and procedures personally because I was involved in several of the jobs, I had regular personal contact with all our employees, and I was frequently on locations. When we expanded to Loving, it was more difficult to monitor compliance but still doable. When we decided to expand to Oklahoma, I knew the people we'd hire wouldn't have prior Wildcat Oil Tools experience and, thus, wouldn't be familiar with our policies and procedures. I also knew I couldn't personally monitor their performance as closely as I had been monitoring our west Texas and New Mexico employees. The question, therefore, was how to make sure our Oklahoma facility did things the Wildcat Oil Tools way. The answer was finding someone who was committed to our Vision and Implementation Plan to head that facility.

I could have promoted someone from our Odessa or Loving yards and had confidence that they would follow our policies and procedures, but I wanted to find someone from Oklahoma. As I've mentioned before, when you're performing fishing and related services, the customer must have confidence in your people or they'll call someone else. I knew it would be significantly easier to develop this confidence if I staffed the Oklahoma yard with people who were working in Oklahoma and were known among Oklahoma oil and gas companies.

Fortunately, I hit a homerun when I found Don Sherrill. Don had spent most of his career working in the oil field in Oklahoma, and he was extremely experienced with rental tools and fishing operations. He knew many of the operators and, more importantly, they trusted him. Don didn't hit the ground running, he hit the ground at a full sprint. Things were slow in Oklahoma at the time and several companies had laid people off. Don hired several good people. Because the local companies trusted Don, they gave us a chance. Don and his crew didn't disappoint.

Don was successful for numerous reasons, including his insistence on doing things right. That ethic dovetailed perfectly with the policies and procedures that I had established. Don trained his people on our policies and procedures and he made sure they did things correctly. Things started slowly, but with a lot of hard work, we built up a base of business, and then steadily grew that base. Ultimately, the first Oklahoma location was so successful that we opened a second yard in Kiowa, Oklahoma. Don performed so well managing these two yards that we eventually transferred him to Odessa to head up our Southern operations.

We continued growing in the US. We opened new facilities and expanded old ones. Before long, we had approximately a dozen locations in four states. Our growth strategy remained consistent throughout this expansion. We talked to our customers to learn where they needed help, and when we identified a potential expansion area, we researched it to see what opportunities were available there. What amount of work could we expect from our existing customers? What other potential customers were in the new area? How much oil and gas activity was taking place now and what level of activity could be expected in the near future? Was there a good location for a shop and yard available? We also looked for someone with local experience that we could hire to run our operations.

Looking back at our growth, it would be easy to say we were aggressive, and in some ways we were, because each new location added risk. It would have been safer to stay with one location and, had we done so, that location would have done well; but it would have meant giving up on our Vision. Don't think we simply expanded for the sake of expansion, however. Each expansion decision was made carefully, thoughtfully, and with as much data as we could assemble. There were times when we considered expansion and after doing the research decided either not to expand to an area or at least not to expand now, because we didn't feel comfortable that the proposed location would succeed. We had to be careful managing our capital investments. Each new location had to carry its own weight quickly because we couldn't afford to subsidize a losing proposition.

Because Wildcat Oil Tools was still a small company, and because we were privately owned, we had the flexibility to act fast and take some risk. This flexibility and risk-tolerance allowed us to take a contrarian approach that was different from our major competitors' approach. For example, when we opened our Pennsylvania yard, we did so at a time when our competitors were leaving the Northeast. They were pulling out because oil prices had dropped, and oil and gas companies had curtailed their drilling plans in response to New York State's fracking ban. We saw an opportunity. There was still plenty of activity in Pennsylvania and its surrounding states, and because of the number of our competitors who had decided to pull out of the Northeast, it appeared to us there would soon be a shortage of service providers.

If I'd been forced to go through all the hoops that I've seen some publicly-traded companies impose on their employees when considering a major decision, or if I had been forced to convince a Board of Directors that Pennsylvania expansion would raise the company's stock price in the next quarter, I probably couldn't have done it. Fortunately, I didn't have to do that. We saw a good opportunity, found a great person to run the Pennsylvania operation, and a wonderful location for a new yard. Because we were moving in when so many others were moving out, we had no trouble finding qualified people with Pennsylvania experience. Their experience and local connections were invaluable.

There is some overlap in the oil and gas companies which were active in Texas, New Mexico, and Oklahoma and, therefore, each time we opened a new location we had existing customers that we could call on. Pennsylvania was largely virgin territory for us, so getting work was a challenge. We had to approach companies that had never heard of us and convince them to make a change from a vendor that they were comfortable with. That invariably requires personal contact. If I had hired people from Texas, New Mexico, or Oklahoma and sent them to Pennsylvania, they would have had a tough time getting in front of potential customers because the customer would have recognized neither our company's name nor our employee's name. However, by hiring good people from the Pennsylvania area, I was starting with employees that our customers knew and trusted. They could get in front of potential customers and introduce them to Wildcat Oil Tools.

CHAPTER 6

We were fortunate with our timing. When we committed ourselves to Pennsylvania, oil prices were low and the overall activity level was depressed, but by the time we were up and running, oil prices had rebounded, and the activity level was picking up. The increased activity coupled with our competitors' departures created a shortage of qualified fishermen, operators, and rental equipment. We happily filled that void and our Pennsylvania yard was not only successful, we eventually had to move to a larger facility to meet the demand.

We followed this same approach to expand our operations throughout the US. We moved into south Texas when others were pulling out and, by doing so, were able to secure a terrific location and talented people. We opened an additional yard in Oklahoma and we bought a small company in east Texas. As I write this chapter, we're looking at other options in the US both by acquiring existing companies with opportunities that complement Wildcat's strengths or that allow us to expand our products and services, and by moving into new markets.

CHAPTER SEVEN

WILDCAT OIL TOOLS' INTERNATIONAL GROWTH

Wildcat Oil Tools followed a similar pattern when we decided to expand internationally. I had traveled internationally several times and was personally comfortable with the notion of doing business in other countries, but I had limited international business experience and few international business contacts. I knew I needed someone with international experience who had contacts with customers, vendors, and potential employees. Ultimately, I found Duane Samford. He had spent several years working for large, multinational service companies. He had the experience and contacts that I needed and, more importantly, he believed in my Vision.

Our international growth was a series of two steps forward, two steps back, and three steps sideways. There were periods of jubilation when we thought we'd found a phenomenal opportunity and periods of disappointment when we discovered we hadn't. Our first big break—or so we thought—occurred when I had a chance meeting with an individual who was responsible for overseeing offshore drilling for a major US oil and gas producer, which was working on a project off the coast of Colombia. I told him that we were expanding our operations internationally. That disclosure led to a conversation about international oil and gas activities. We hit it off, and he invited us to participate in their project as a vendor.

We thought at the time that we had hit a homerun and we hit the ground running. My new friend introduced us to several people in his company, we toured one of their offshore drilling platforms, and we were introduced to an influential businessperson in Colombia who was looking for US businesses like ours to work with. This businessperson was able to help us out with logistical issues such as warehouse space and local employees. Our general counsel established a Colombian subsidiary for our operations. Duane worked on the business arrangements. I looked for additional Colombian opportunities. Having a contract in Colombia with one major company would allow us to get our foot in the door, but to have a successful overseas entity we knew we needed to work for several other companies as well.

Eventually we traveled to Bogotá to meet with potential customers, bankers, lawyers, and accountants. I love Bogotá. Because of what you see on television, most Americans assume Colombia is incredibly dangerous and, therefore, taking a business trip to Bogotá is extremely risky. Nothing could be further from the truth. The people are terrific. They're friendly, warm, and helpful. I've always been comfortable and felt safe in Bogotá. We typically stay at an American-owned hotel that looks exactly like our American hotels, we frequently walk to meetings or for dinner, and we use Uber when we need a ride. Bogotá is a large city, so there's always plenty to see

CHAPTER 7

and do. We've never experienced any trouble, let alone encountered a dangerous situation.

Unfortunately, the trip to Bogotá took a lot of the wind out of our sails, because we learned there simply wasn't enough activity to justify a big investment. Colombia has tremendous potential, but they haven't adopted all the completion techniques that US companies are using, such as fracking, to dramatically increase domestic oil and gas production. Consequently, they haven't drilled nearly as many wells as we have and there wasn't as much demand for our tools and services as we would have preferred. Our Colombian business model also took a hit when the major that we had been working with decided to delay their Colombian offshore drilling activities because of low energy prices. We were eventually able to do some work in Colombia, but it was minimal and periodic. However, this allowed us to say we were now an international company, and the process was instructive.

Every country is unique; however, there are similar issues that must be overcome when you decide to expand internationally. For example, how will I get my products into the country? What taxes or import fees will I owe if I import equipment? What taxes must I pay on my revenue? What are the local employment laws? How do I get currency into or out of the country? Do I have to set up an entity in the country or can I conduct business through a local representative or other arrangement? Dealing with each of these issues in Colombia made our other international expansions easier because we had a better idea what to expect and, just as we had adopted protocols for domestic expansion, we started developing protocols for international expansion.

Our next effort was in the United Arab Emirates (UAE). We were introduced to an individual with a small service company who had opportunities to expand, but who lacked the capital to do so, and who wanted to sell a portion of his company to raise capital. The opportunity was intriguing because the seller had contracts that guaranteed a baseline of business, he had started the process of qualifying to do business with Saudi Aramco, and he was approved by them for product testing. It appeared to us that his upside was good and could be realistically achieved with a reasonable capital infusion. Buying into an existing business would save us considerable time and expense if for no other reason because we would then have all of the required permits and licenses and would be in business in the UAE the day the deal closed. More importantly, we had every expectation of being able to do business with Aramco shortly thereafter.

We traveled to the UAE to meet with the seller and his representative. We liked the seller and were impressed with his representative. This individual had grown up in Houston and attended college at the University of Texas. He was, therefore, intimately familiar with the customs in both the US and Middle East. Our conversations with the seller went well and we entered into a preliminary agreement. Our general counsel started work on the definitive purchase agreement and our due diligence review.

Problems are to be expected during the due diligence process, and this transaction was no exception. We had been previously told that the seller disliked and distrusted attorneys and, therefore, didn't want to spend time on formal legal tasks or contracts. As a fellow businessperson, I could understand his general desire to minimize legal expenses and avoid unnecessary paperwork. During our trip to the UAE, the seller shared stories of past difficulties that he attributed to attorneys making everything unnecessarily difficult. He also stressed how important it was that this be treated as the simple, straightforward deal that, in his opinion, it was. His story seemed plausible, so I wasn't concerned about simplifying things. Our general counsel didn't give up on wanting to perform a due diligence review of the company, but he worked hard to simplify the paperwork.

Fortunately for us, before we irrevocably committed ourselves to the deal, we discovered that the seller's company owed a vendor a considerable sum of money because he had been careless. The seller should have disclosed this liability, and it helped explain his prior reluctance to provide us with records and access to his business information. The seller was afraid that if he had disclosed the liability earlier, it would have scuttled the deal and he was hoping that he could use our purchase money to reach a settlement agreement with the vendor without us ever being aware of the issue. However, the vendor found out that we were negotiating a deal to buy a portion of the company, and refused to negotiate with the seller but, instead, insisted on full payment. When we learned about the extent of the claim, we immediately cancelled the transaction.

The irony is that if the seller had disclosed this outstanding claim at the beginning of our discussions, it might nevertheless have killed the deal, but not immediately. Wildcat Oil Tools would have first approached the vendor to discuss a business resolution. We had done business with that particular vendor, so it's possible that they would have negotiated an agreement because of our prior relationship and the opportunity to grow that relationship. Unfortunately, the seller made a poor decision because the mere fact that this claim hadn't been disclosed in a timely manner was enough to kill the deal. You have to trust the people you do business with and you should never do business with someone you don't trust. I have no doubt that the seller is a good man who made a mistake. However, I didn't want to risk Wildcat Oil Tools' name, let alone our capital, if there was any question about other undisclosed problems, or any concern that future problems might not be disclosed in a timely manner.

Fortunately, there was a silver lining to the cloud. As I noted, we liked the seller's representative and, as it turns out, this representative was impressed with us, too. In some countries, a foreign company can do business by appointing a local representative. That can be an attractive option because it's simpler than creating a foreign subsidy. After the deal fell apart, the seller's representative contacted us to see if we would be willing to work with him. He couldn't do anything in the UAE that would conflict with his duties to the seller, but he could represent us elsewhere and he knew of several opportunities.

We talked and eventually entered into a contract with his company, Al Mazroui Trading and General Services. They helped us secure a contract to provide drilling equipment for a project in Kuwait. The contract wasn't big, but it gave us a footprint in the Middle East and, therefore, made it easier to expand to other Middle Eastern countries. In addition, the contract allowed us to say that we were now operational on three continents.

In the Middle East, having a contract with Saudi Aramco is essential. First, their high level of activity creates numerous opportunities. Second, because they are widely respected in the region, being able to say that you are an Aramco vendor gives you instant credibility. Conversely, having to admit that you aren't an Aramco vendor undercuts your credibility. Al Mazroui's affiliation helped us here because they were well known and respected by Aramco officials.

The first big hurdle that we had to clear was Aramco's foreign experience requirement. Aramco requires foreign companies to have at least five years of international experience before they will consider working with you. There are, however, exceptions for companies with new technology. Through our research and development efforts, we had developed proprietary tools and could show they had been successfully used in the US and South America. We could also establish that our tools were better than anything Aramco was using. We were able to get an audience with Aramco officials, and we traveled to Saudi Arabia and to pitch our proprietary products. The Aramco officials listened, liked what they heard, and invited us to participate in product testing. Their invitation allowed us a chance to win a contract even though we didn't have five years of international experience.

During our trip, we also learned the importance of ISO certification for international business transactions. ISO 9001 is a set of international standards for quality management systems. ISO certification isn't ordinarily required in US transactions because our customers would rather look at our quality management system directly. We learned, however, that many of our potential international clients wanted their vendors to have ISO certification.

Fortunately, Wildcat Oil Tools' quality management system was state of the art because of the world-class policies and procedures that I had insisted that Wildcat Oil Tools follow from day one. As a result, we didn't have to develop new quality management processes; instead, we simply had to go through the certification process. Thanks to some hard work by our folks, we finished that process quickly and received our certification.

About this same time, we also secured a wonderful opportunity in Argentina. We had worked with Deep Well Services on several Pennsylvania projects. Deep Well is a service company that provides services which are complementary to ours. It's a well-run company and I always enjoyed working with its people. Deep Well had an opportunity to work with AESA, an Argentina oil company and they asked Wildcat Oil Tools if we would be interested in participating. AESA wanted Deep Well to provide a wide range of equipment and services, some of which Deep Well didn't provide but which Wildcat Oil Tools did.

We looked at the proposed package and were interested enough to explore it further. We met with AESA and YPF executives in the US. AESA is a wholly-owned subsidiary of YPF, which in turn is owned by the Argentinian government. That meeting went well, and, as a result, we lined up a trip to Argentina. The potential AESA contract was tempting, but we knew in order to have a successful Argentina operation, we had to have more than one contract. We also had concerns about some of the practical problems we would encounter if we opened a permanent facility in Argentina, such as employment issues, banking, and taxes.

The trip was a complete success. We were warmly welcomed by Argentinian officials, labor union representatives, and potential customers. We had heard horror stories about being unable to take currency out of the country and about the difficulty of working with the local unions. The Argentinian officials and local lawyers that we met with were able to address many of those concerns. Argentina's

CHAPTER 7

government has undertaken numerous reforms in the last ten years that have made it much easier for US-based companies to operate in Argentina. The labor union representatives we met with displayed a willingness to work with us if we could provide their members a safe working environment. Finally, several privately owned companies promised to provide us with work and expressed a willingness to offer us incentives to invest in an Argentinian operation.

We decided to move forward and we entered into contract negotiations with YPF and AESA. We also set up a Wildcat Oil Tools subsidiary in Argentina. We added Miguel Di Vincenzo as Vice President for South America. Miguel had a great deal of prior experience in South America and he knew a number of key people. His experience opened a lot of doors for us and allowed us to expand in Argentina more efficiently. Di Vincenzo's experience and contacts allowed us to enter into a comprehensive contract with YPF and to establish a viable presence in Argentina, and also gave us the credibility to approach other vendors.

When you run a business in the US, you may not be politically active, but you monitor political developments, such as taxes, regulations, or incentives, that can impact your business. When you're involved in international business, you must monitor political developments in several countries. During this time period, we were looking at expanding into Mexico, but we had to shelve that effort when Andrés Manual López Obrador won the Mexican presidential election and shortly thereafter effectively banned fracking. Our Argentinian expansion became more problematic when President Mauricio Macri's party did poorly in primary elections and we had to consider what impact a new president might have on Argentinian business practices.

I wish that I had a simple, foolproof solution to eliminate the uncertainty inherent in international politics, but unfortunately, I don't. We were always aware of the risk and we constantly looked for ways to minimize the disruption to our business that would be caused if a new administration took office and fundamentally changed oil and gas exploration activities, employment or tax laws, or currency transfer laws. We did have one key advantage over much of our competition. Because Wildcat Oil Tools was comparatively small and privately owned, we could be nimble. If the business environment in country X changed dramatically, in a way that was negative to our interests, we could quickly shift our investment to another country.

We worked hard to retain this flexibility. When Wildcat Oil Tools made international investment decisions, we not only considered the economics of the purchase—what rate of return could we reasonably expect and whether there were better investment opportunities—we also considered how this impacted our footprint. For example, if we needed a facility to store and maintain equipment which also had offices for our people, we could normally purchase or rent an industrial building with yard space. We would perform standard financial calculations to determine if we could cover the facility's cost with our expected revenue and if the capital expenditure was otherwise a good investment. We also considered what if's, such as what if the political climate changed and we no longer wanted to maintain a presence in that country? Owning a facility might make better sense financially than renting but if we wanted to leave, we'd have to sell that facility. That consideration restricted our flexibility and was, therefore, a factor in the decision whether to buy or to rent.

These and similar issues had to be addressed each time we expanded our international footprint or considered an additional investment. However, we persevered, and, as of this writing, Wildcat Oil Tools has operations on three continents and we are working on opportunities on two other continents.

CHAPTER EIGHT

WILDCAT OIL TOOLS' GROWTH IN PRODUCTS AND SERVICES

No area of the company has grown faster than our products. As I write this, Wildcat Oil Tools has grown from four BOPs to seventy-three different product lines. Several more are under development.

Originally, our product line growth was purely organic, occurring without a comprehensive, strategic Plan. As I've noted, I kept my original list of products on a yellow pad. I added products when a customer called, and asked, "Do you have an X?" If I didn't have an X, but I thought that I could keep it rented, I bought one and added it to the list. Our initial services complemented our existing products directly. By that I mean that when you rented a pump, for example, we provided an operator to run it. For much of the same reason, we added fishing services early in our history because, at the time, the people who were renting our equipment were frequently engaged in fishing operations.

We could have continued following this model, and, had we done so, we would have grown; however, we would never have distinguished ourselves from our competition, because multiple companies were renting the same products and providing the same services. Sooner or later, this lack of distinction would have capped our growth potential. That lack of growth was completely counter to my Vision. Consequently, we made a series of strategic decisions that not only allowed us to achieve our goal of becoming a world-class service company, but also helped us focus our growth.

One of those decisions was to develop our own proprietary tools. I've previously discussed the development of our research and development program and how it separated us from most of our competition because so few of them engaged in research and development. When you strictly sell and rent off-the-shelf products built by third parties, it's difficult to control your destiny. If a customer wants to rent a pump and you're one of several companies that rent the exact same pump, why should they choose you? If you can only provide services because you offer them at a lower price, you put yourself in a dangerous box. When times are slow, you have to discount your prices so much to get, or even to keep, business, that you aren't profitable. Consequently, at Wildcat Oil Tools, we wanted our own tools that were superior to anything else on the market, so that our sales representatives had a selling point other than price. To help grow our bottom line, these products also needed to complement our current operations, so that we could offer them as an add-on.

Our first proprietary tool was a wellbore cleaning tool, the HydroVortex. This tool is used to remove debris, such as sand and stones, from a wellbore. It was far better than anything else on the market. Normally, while drilling or working on a well, the operator pumps fluid down the drill pipe to the bottom of the wellbore. Because the operator continues pumping fluid, this fluid is then circulated to the surface in the space between the pipe and wellbore. Normally, that fluid picks up any loose debris and brings it to the surface. Sometimes, however, the operator has poor circulation because of mechanical issues in the wellbore, and, as a result, sand and other materials begin to collect and eventually block off the producing formation. Our HydroVortex acts like a vacuum cleaner. Even in a wellbore with poor circulation, we can use it to capture loose debris and bring it to the surface.

The HydroVortex was a good fit for us because frequently we were already out on location fishing when an operator needed help removing debris from a wellbore. We could offer our HydroVortex as an immediate solution to the problem. It's easy for an operator to say "yes" when you're offering an immediate solution. The HydroVortex worked well and received tremendous reviews from our customers. That success made it easier for us to market the HydroVortex to new customers.

We expanded and shifted our research and development department when other opportunities presented themselves. For example, I learned about an engineer with a well-earned reputation for tool design. He was responsible for numerous patents and had been working with a larger company. He had an idea for a new whipstock design. A whipstock is a tool that oil companies use when they want to drill a hole directionally—for example, when they start drilling horizontally. His employer wasn't interested in pursuing that design, so he came to work for us. We staffed up to design and develop the whipstock. Ultimately, it became the Wildcat XpressDrill.

The HydroVortex complemented our fishing operations because it was a remedial tool: that is, it was a tool frequently used in connection with fishing operations. The XpressDrill could also be used on a fishing job if the company decided that rather than continuing trying to clear or repair a wellbore, it would simply drill around the problem; but it was our first drilling tool. This new tool was a big development for our company and one that is more significant than it might appear if you're unfamiliar with oil and gas operations.

Oil companies normally use one division to drill wells and a separate division to operate them because the two tasks require different equipment and skill sets. Our experience and contacts were with the operating divisions. Thus, even though Wildcat Oil Tools had done work for Company X for years, their drilling department may have never heard of us. We had to spend considerable time developing new relationships and establishing credibility.

Fortunately, we made headway and were able to expand our drilling tools. We next developed a frac plug. A frac plug, as its name suggests, is used by oil companies when they frac a well. Frac plugs allow oil companies to isolate a portion of a wellbore by setting plugs on each end of the area that they want to fracture. The operator pressures up the space between the two plugs. That pressure escapes the wellbore through previously-made small holes in the casing, and then it fractures the adjacent oil-containing rock. Those fractures free the oil and allow it to flow into the wellbore.

Because we now had established relationships with drilling departments, we knew who to talk to and we had a much easier time getting an audience. The challenge with many new tools—frac plugs are a prime example—is convincing someone to risk their multi-million dollar well with a new tool. Fortunately, we had good test data and good field trial data, and a couple of customers gave us a chance. Successful runs on their wells gave us credibility and made it easier to convince others to give us a chance. Our frac plug was so well-designed that all we needed was a chance, because its performance guaranteed future orders.

During this time period we modified our product growth strategy. We had always been careful to add new products that complimented our current products, and to listen to our customers when they described their wants and needs. While listening to customers, we learned that several of our larger customers wanted to reduce the number of vendors on a location at any one point in time. For almost any product or service that an oil company will want during the drilling, completion, or operation of a well, they will have at least one vendor that is a specialist in that area and at least one vendor that provides the needed product or service as part of a larger inventory of products and services.

I can make an excellent argument for using either a generalist or a specialist vendor. For example, if I need a widget and I call a company that sells nothing but widgets, chances are pretty good that they know what they're doing, that I'll get the right widget, and it will be installed correctly. On the other hand, a generalist vendor can frequently offer lower prices because their overhead can be divided over several products and services.

Our customers were concerned about both quality and prices, but for many, the motivating factor was safety. When the number of vendors on a location increases, so does the chances of an accident because it becomes more difficult to coordinate everyone's actions. Fortunately, this concern gave us a tremendous opportunity.

Prior to starting Wildcat Oil Tools, my background was in safety. I brought that Mindset with me to Wildcat Oil Tools. My insistence on adopting and following world-class protocols made us a safer company. Our safety record is one of the best in the business. Thus, when a customer mentioned a need to make changes to their vendor list for safety reasons, we could respond that first, we were a safe company with a superior safety record and, therefore, having us on location would automatically help prevent accidents. Secondly, our product growth allowed us to offer a wide range of products and services, thus reducing the number of vendors they would otherwise need.

To better position ourselves, we started looking around job sites when we were on location to see who else was present. We'd then find out what products and services they were providing and would ask ourselves if these were something that we wanted to offer. If so, we added it. We started using the slogan "One Call, Many Solutions."

This openness to new products led us to add wireline and thru tubing services. Wireline refers to using a high-grade cable to lower tools and instruments into a wellbore. The cable is electrical, so you can use it to operate specialized measuring instruments. We refer to this type of operation as "logging." For example, we can measure the density of a formation and its shale content. We can also determine whether the cement behind the casing is present and if it has properly set. Wireline trucks can also set frac plugs and then drill them out after a well has been fracked.

CHAPTER 8

Because wireline is used for so many different things, it allowed us to cross-market. For example, if a customer was using one of our trucks while fracking a well, it gave us the opportunity to sell them our plug. On the other hand, if a customer was using our frac plug, that gave us a chance to market our wireline trucks. We looked for other opportunities to cross-market by expanding our inventory of wireline-operated tools, frequently referred to as thru tubing tools. We bought standard thru tubing tools for general operations, and added proprietary new tools, such as an improved downhole motor, when the opportunity presented itself.

We also took advantage of opportunities to utilize our yard space more efficiently. One example of efficiency was the addition of a machine shop. The pipe that oil companies use to drill, complete, and operate wells is reused when possible. Before it can be reused, the pipe must be inspected and if the threads at the end of the pipe are damaged, they must be recut. Our fishing and wireline work was often performed on wells that were being plugged and we helped customers recover reusable pipe before the well was plugged. Because we were already helping recover the pipe, it only made sense to also have the ability to inspect and repair it, so we added a machine shop and pipe yard at our Odessa facility.

I started this chapter by noting that we've grown from a single product line to over seventy lines. By the time you read this, we'll have several more. The growth has been phenomenal, and it's been exciting to have been part of it. However, rather than go through each addition, I'm going to shift now from Wildcat Oil Tools' history and return to how you can use the tools and processes that I've used to grow Wildcat Oil Tools to accomplish your organization's Vision.

CHAPTER NINE
VISION DISCIPLINE AND EXECUTING THE PLAN

I started this book setting out the three keys to visionary leadership: Vision, Plan, and Mindset. So far, I've primarily discussed my Vision and Wildcat Oil Tools' history, with a brief detour to consider Mindset. I'm now going to concentrate on the second key, the Implementation Plan. The Implementation Plan converts your Vision from a goal to a reality. Of the three elements, it's the hardest to achieve, because it requires good old-fashioned hard work and self-discipline. The good news is that when an Implementation Plan is properly developed and implemented, it has the greatest opportunity to separate you from your competition.

I once saw "discipline" described as choosing what you want most over what you want now. When your organization is focused on a Vision, a certain amount of organizational discipline automatically takes hold. When we committed ourselves to making Wildcat Oil Tools the premier fishing and tool rental company in the world, that commitment alone informed decisions large and small. We knew what the world's premier fishing and tool rental company would look and act like. We started modeling ourselves to fit that Vision rather than the reality which our circumstances would have suggested at the time.

Modeling ourselves with a picture far more ambitious than our current circumstances was immediately more consequential than it may sound because it separated Wildcat Oil Tools from the competition and it prevented us from being held back by a glass ceiling. There are innumerable small service companies in the oil and gas industry. Typically, these are referred to as "mom-and-pop" companies. When we started, and indeed for our first few years, we were the classic mom-and-pop company: humble facilities, off-the-shelf product lines, and closely-held ownership. It would have been perfectly logical, therefore, for our employees and customers to have seen us as a mom-and-pop company and for us to have acted like one. Had we done so we would have never achieved the growth that we managed to obtain.

Before I go any further, please understand there is nothing wrong with a mom-and-pop service company or any other type of small business. I know of many small service companies that are well-run and successful. In fact, I routinely recommend several of these to others and I haven't hesitated to work with small start-ups myself; but a mom-and-pop service company has a ceiling to which I didn't want to limit myself. For example, mom-and-pop service companies do not engage in international business transactions or develop proprietary tools.

In business, the label people use to describe your organization is critically important because it defines you. There was no escaping the fact that we were a small start-up, but it was important that people saw us as a growing company with unlimited potential. When a company such as ours gets labeled as a mom-and-pop, it's extremely difficult to overcome the limitations that label imposes. For example, some of the larger customers we were targeting had stringent vendor requirements including a favorable reputation for handling large, complex projects; consequently, being known as a mom-and-pop business would have made it far more difficult, if not impossible, for us to get some of the work we were ultimately able to obtain. It was, thus, critical that we always looked, acted, and felt like an internationally-acclaimed company, even if that notion was somewhat fanciful at the beginning.

To give you an idea of how the commitment to a Vision influenced our strategic decision making, consider our tool inventory. Anyone can start a fishing and tool rental company and completely stock itself with off-the-shelf tools. There are several well-known and well-regarded tool manufacturers. As long as we bought good tools and equipment from respected manufacturers and we maintained them, no customer would ever think twice about using us simply because our operators and fishermen were using off-the-shelf tools and equipment. However, a world-class service company has its own proprietary tools and equipment.

No one would have ever criticized Wildcat Oil Tools as an organization if we had never attempted to design and manufacture our own tools. Many of the oilfield tools currently in use have been around for years. Developing a new tool design, testing it, patenting it, and then successfully marketing it is inherently expensive and risky. However, when you can pull that feat off, the fact that you did so dramatically and unequivocally separates you from the competition.

I remember attending a meeting hosted by one of our publicly-traded customers with its vendors to discuss their upcoming plans. During this meeting a question was asked of the group: who has a research and development department? We were the only non-publicly-traded company to raise our hand. That was a special moment for me. The looks that we got were priceless. Our competitors were chagrined, our customer smiled, and others looked at us wondering, "Who are these guys?" We couldn't help but puff our chests out and stand a little taller.

Let me get back to how a Vision provided Wildcat Oil Tools with strategic discipline. We decided to add a research and development department because the world's premier fishing and tool rental company would have one. The idea truly was that simple. Because we weren't worried about whether we should or shouldn't have a research and development program, we were able to focus our time and energy on developing a Plan and recruiting talent. This Vision also freed Wildcat's team from any self-doubt about the wisdom of starting the program. That focus gave us more confidence than we probably should have had, but a firmly-held belief in your ultimate success can become a self-fulfilling prophecy.

While our Vision provided some discipline, don't allow yourself to think that a Vision alone supplies all the discipline that your organization will ever need to achieve it. You must also have a comprehensive, well thought out Implementation Plan. I can't emphasize the importance of your Implementation Plan. In fact, it's my firm belief that a Vision without a Plan is simply wishful thinking. Thomas Edison is credited with saying that genius is 1 percent inspiration and 99 percent perspiration. That breakdown is

CHAPTER 9

definitely true in the business world. The Vision is what everyone remembers, and developing a Vision is fun. The Implementation Plan, however, is what makes the Vision reality. Rest assured, developing a Plan is work. Implementing that Plan is even more work. Sticking with the Plan is hard work.

In Wildcat Oil Tools' case, the Implementation Plan consisted, first, of the written job processes that I discussed earlier. I knew we had to look and act like a world-class company. So, we developed written processes for each of the tasks that we performed for our customers. Those processes were the same ones that the major service companies were using, and they both helped us look like what we wanted to become and separated us from our competition. These processes also improved our quality management system. Because we knew our processes worked, insisting our employees follow them faithfully eliminated a lot of mistakes. That consistency not only improved our work quality, it prevented accidents and injuries. Consequently, we were a better and safer company because of our adherence to established job processes.

The oil and gas industry is, unfortunately, dangerous to work in. The equipment we work with and around is large and heavy, much of it moves, and some of it is elevated. We frequently work with highly-pressured hot fluids and gases. We work outside 365 days a year, twenty-four hours a day. Each of these factors imposes risks on the people who work on location. To address these risk factors, every oil company has a safety program in place, and accident histories are tracked. When we approach a new customer, one of the first things they ask about is our accident history and our safety rating.

I'm proud to say our safety rating is outstanding. That commitment to safety opened a lot of doors for us.

Our Implementation Plan also accounted for future growth, both in locations and product lines. I didn't have a comprehensive list of future locations or product lines when we first started, but we definitely intended to grow, and as we developed, we were already positioned to consider the locations and products that would complement our existing locations and products. Our Implementation Plan also addressed our financing. Early on, we decided we wanted Wildcat Oil Tools to remain privately owned so that we could retain operational control. So, we focused on ways to raise capital without resorting to private equity markets.

As we continued to grow, the Implementation Plans became more sophisticated. Our written job processes, for example, became part of a comprehensive quality management and quality control program. My yellow pad list of our products and prices was incorporated into a sophisticated accounting program. Multi-page carbonless invoices were replaced with a customized and computerized ticketing and invoicing system. Even as we grew, however, the core tenants of the Implementation Plan never changed because our Vision never changed.

We couldn't have achieved our Vision without that Implementation Plan. Neither can you. Visions do not take care of themselves. Without leadership's continued commitment to the Implementation Plan, the organization's path to the Vision starts to look like a ship without a rudder attempting to navigate to a particular destination. The ship might get there, but if it does, its arrival is probably an accident. Visions can, and will, help steer your organization in a

CHAPTER 9

strategic direction. They will not solve every problem and, in fact, when challenges arise—and they will—sticking to the Vision will often make problem-solving more difficult because you'll have to resist the temptation to compromise your Vision by taking an easy out. If the organization's leadership sticks to the Plan, however, and reinforces the Vision when these inevitable problems arise, you'll ultimately see that commitment reflected in the organization's day-to-day discipline. Your job as a leader, therefore, is to take control of the Implementation Plan and to lead by example.

Leading by example can be a difficult job that requires considerable discipline. Every business has its ups and downs. In the oil and gas industry, these fluctuations are frequently associated with commodity prices. For example, when oil or gas prices rise, more wells are drilled and there is greater need for drilling tools and support services. That need increases our activity level and income. When oil or gas prices decrease, companies cut back on their drilling plans and maintenance programs. Fewer wells mean less need for drilling tools and support services. Reduced maintenance programs mean less demand for our remedial products and services. That reduction, in turn, lowers our income. There is nothing that I can do to influence the price of oil or gas. I can, however, direct our response to the inevitable price swings.

It's easy to see how difficult times require discipline to stick to your Plan, but good times can be just as challenging. When times are good, it's tempting to relax and reward yourself even if that detracts from your Implementation Plan. After all, your success is surely a sign that you deserve it and you promise yourself you'll be more disciplined tomorrow after this reward. This temptation to relax is like saying, "Just one dessert" while you're on a diet. How often have you managed to eat one dessert and then successfully get back on the diet? Similarly, when business is slow, it's tempting to disregard the Implementation Plan and cut corners to minimize your costs. This is a particularly easy decision to rationalize because times are tough, and besides, when things get better, you'll be able to get back to the Plan. Maybe you will, but realistically isn't more likely that the lowered standards will become the new normal?

Conversely, if you lead by example and demonstrate discipline at these key moments, how much more likely is it that your Vision and your Implementation Plan will become a part of the organization's DNA? Let me give you an example. In 2016, the stock market crash impacted Wildcat Oil Tools as it impacted everyone else. The oil and gas industry as a whole suffered. Our access to capital took a hit. We could have justified cutting corners and curtailing our plans. Instead, we took advantage of the situation by moving into areas out of which our competition was pulling. Their departures left holes that we could fill, while the general slowdown made prime yard locations available. We needed capital to fund this growth, and that put a lot of financial stress on the company. Every capital investment had to be well thought out and precise because we had no margin for error. I don't mean we had little margin for error—I mean we had *none*. We couldn't afford to purchase equipment that wasn't going to be rented and paying for itself quickly or to hire employees who wouldn't be busy. We were doubling down by expanding at a time when everyone else was contracting. That risk-taking gave us opportunities that would have otherwise been unavailable, but we had to pay for it.

CHAPTER 9

The investments required by Wildcat's growth challenged our Implementation Plan. Prior to the stock market crash, the oil and gas industry had done well because of high commodity prices. That had led to the creation of several service businesses offering products and services similar to ours. Many of those failed to survive. When a service company went under, they or their lender would try to sell equipment to competitors and would auction off any remaining equipment. I was contacted numerous times by people offering used tools and equipment at a discount. Frequently this was equipment that I absolutely had to have to stock our new locations or keep up with demand at our existing locations.

Our Implementation Plan included purchasing new equipment because we could better control the quality of our services if we utilized equipment that was properly serviced and maintained, but the chance to save money by buying surplus equipment was tempting. By 2015, we had expanded to Houston and Midland, Texas; Loving, New Mexico; and Oklahoma City, Oklahoma. In 2016, we added a yard in Carmichaels, Pennsylvania. Each new yard needed a great deal of expensive equipment, such as fishing tools, pumps, and BOPs. Each new yard had to be staffed with high-quality people. Each new yard also needed pickup trucks, computers, printers, and on and on. At the same time, of course, our existing yards were growing and they also needed some of the equipment that we were getting for the new yards.

Our substantial need for expensive new equipment at a time of low oil and gas prices challenged my commitment to our Implementation Plan tremendously. With the squeeze we were facing, I could have easily justified cutting corners to stretch our capital budget. I remember, for example, a pump purchase. We use expensive, highly-specialized pumps for our operations. Those pumps serve a critical role for our customers. When they need one, it has to work, because if that pump goes out, the project halts until the pump is repaired or replaced. Downtime costs customers a lot of money because they're paying every other vendor on location to do nothing but wait. Customers are therefore concerned about the quality of our pumps. We take a great deal of pride in our pump fleet. We buy good pumps, we maintain those pumps, and we can fully document each of our pump's histories because we're that pump's only owner.

In 2016, I needed several pumps both to stock the new yards and to meet increased customer demands at the older yards. At the time, a new pump cost me $200,000. I was being contacted and offered surplus pumps for $10,000. The surplus pumps were the same type as the ones that we were using. Do the math. I could have bought twenty used pumps for the price of one new pump. It would have been extremely easy to rationalize buying surplus pumps, or any of the other equipment that was offered to me, because I would have saved a small fortune, and I definitely could have used the savings to fund other capital expenditures. However, I couldn't buy surplus equipment from failed service companies and stay true to our Implementation Plan.

Quality equipment was a key component of our Plan. An oil company isn't going to risk its investment in a well by using a service company that it doesn't trust. That trust includes trust in the service company's people and its equipment. Price is important, and our customers are always looking for ways to control costs. When you're

CHAPTER 9

seriously ill, however, do you pick the cheapest doctor that you can find, or do you look for one who you have confidence in? We had grown precisely because our customers trusted us with their multi-million-dollar investments. We would have jeopardized that trust by showing up on location with salvaged equipment. In addition, I couldn't expect my people to continue acting like they belonged to a world-class company if I equipped them with salvaged equipment.

We decided to forgo the offers of great deals on surplus equipment. Even though I knew that it was the right decision, there were still times when I questioned myself. For example, when we were working with the books and were considering the ever-increasing capital requests, there were frequently times when it felt like our equipment needs were greater than we could possibly fund. In those moments, I couldn't help but consider if buying some salvaged equipment instead of new wouldn't solve the day's problems. Of course, I always assured myself that this was a temporary move and that when I got caught up, I'd start buying new equipment again. Truth be told, in any given month or quarter, cutting a corner would have solved the problem of the day, but we always refused. Today we're unquestionably a better company and in better shape because we didn't ignore our Vision and Implementation Plan to solve a temporary problem.

Even so, this commitment wasn't without consequence. We had a finite amount of capital. When I spent $200,000 on a new pump, instead of $10,000 on a used one, that meant that I didn't have $190,000 for other items. All of my yard managers had legitimate needs for additional or replacement equipment and supplies, as well as more staff. I've been fortunate to have managers who treat our capital as if it was their own money. They don't come to me with unreasonable requests. If they told me that they needed something, I knew they did. Nonetheless, I was frequently forced to say "no" or "not now." We also weren't able to provide the bonuses and raises that I wanted to give and which our people deserved. As you can see, I frequently had to disappoint my own people.

The only reason that I had the discipline to stick with the Implementation Plan was my firm belief that short-term disappointment would more than be offset by future reward. A commercial that I like shows a father and son turning a coffee can into a piggy bank. As part of this process, they put a piece of tape on the can and write the word "glove" on it. Thereafter, every coin or bill that the son puts in the can gets him closer to his goal of having a new baseball glove. The commercial then shows the young man using that same process several years later to save for bigger purchases such as a new couch. The idea is that having a clear goal made it easier to save money.

The same holds true for companies. I assume the young man who was saving money for a baseball glove was periodically tempted to spend some of his money on other things. The coffee-can piggy bank helped him exercise discipline because it reminded him of his goal. If a friend invited him to go see a new movie and he would need to raid the piggy bank to go, he would be reminded why he was saving money and would then presumably ask himself which was more important: getting the new glove or seeing the movie? Our Implementation Plan made it easier—or at least less difficult—for me to say "no" when that was the right thing to do.

CHAPTER 9

When someone asked me to make a capital purchase and I said "no" or "not now," I wasn't doing it to hurt anyone's feelings or to show the world who was the boss. I said "no" because I believed the money they were asking for would better serve our Vision if spent elsewhere. Obviously, some people were disappointed when I said "No," but as long as it was clear that I was committed to our Vision and Implementation Plan, and that my decisions were fueled by that commitment, they were far less likely to take it personally. If my actions consistently confirmed that commitment, I achieved greater buy-in from my managers.

My managers, all of them team players, were doing their job by looking out for their areas of responsibility. They all had needs and problems and were looking to me for help. When they realized how committed I was to the Implementation Plan, they gained an appreciation for how that Plan would bring about our Vision and they committed themselves to the process. They didn't just ask themselves what they needed to make their lives easier; instead, they considered whether a request was consistent with our Plan and Vision and, if it wasn't, they reconsidered that request before coming to me.

Buy-in from my senior managers was critical because without it, the Wildcat Oil Tools team couldn't have executed our Plan, which leads me to another point. I don't want you thinking I was sitting on a throne making these difficult decisions by myself. I was blessed to have a strong chief financial officer (CFO) and supportive partners. Not only did my team support me when I needed it, it was an important part of the decision-making process, which sometimes meant telling me "no" when I needed to hear that.

As your organization grows, you, too, will need a core team to help you, because you cannot be an expert at everything. I don't care how talented you are, everyone has weaknesses. The key is to identify yours and then address them. How you do so will depend on your weaknesses and your resources. For example, if you're just starting and you have trouble making sales calls because of a lack of confidence, you may consider working with a mentor or practicing with friends. As your organization grows, addressing your weaknesses will often require hiring people who are experts in a field that's not your strength. While this insight sounds obvious, it's surprising how often people have trouble hiring someone who is smarter than they are or more talented in a specific area. Fortunately, I've never had any trouble bringing on people who knew more than I did, because I've never felt as if I had to be the smartest person in the room; I just wanted to make sure that person is on my side.

I have a business degree, but I'm not a financial or tax wizard, and I need help from people who are experts in those areas. When we first started Wildcat Oil Tools, our books were little more than a computerized check register. We kept up with the money coming in and the money going out using a simple, off-the-shelf bookkeeping program. When bills came in, they were reviewed and placed in a stack. When we billed a customer, we kept a copy of our invoice in a separate stack until it was paid. The nice thing about this system is that I could quickly look at those two stacks and the balance in our checking account to see how well we were doing. We transferred paid bills and invoices to paper files. At the end of the year, we took these files to our accountant to prepare a tax return.

CHAPTER 9

In the beginning, this rudimentary system worked. When Wildcat Oil Tools started growing, the accounting challenges exploded. Additional employees meant more payroll and payroll tax issues. Those issues are bad enough when your business operates in one state. They double when you expand to a second state because the laws are different enough from each other to create a headache. You can imagine what happens when you expand into several states, let alone different countries. More equipment means additional depreciation schedules. Increased activity means additional bills and invoices. Each new location requires additional tax filings.

My sister and I couldn't handle this challenge by ourselves. She was already stretched trying to keep up, and we could see the volume was only going to increase. I couldn't help her because I didn't have the background or the time. I knew without a doubt that I could serve Wildcat Oil Tools far better by getting out of the office and talking to customers, managers, and employees. I didn't like the idea of adding to my overhead by hiring a non-revenue-producing employee, but fortunately I did the smart thing. I went out and hired a CFO, Gina Berrones.

Gina is one of the major reasons why we achieved our Vision. I know I keep referring to individual people this way, but it's the truth. An organization is unquestionably more than the sum of its parts. Without Gina, a hole would have precluded us from advancing beyond a small company. She was experienced, and she knew her job. When she assumed the CFO role, her knowledge and experience immediately made Wildcat Oil Tools more sophisticated. Our new accounting processes allowed us to continue growing and to expand our areas of operation.

Not only did Gina bring expertise to Wildcat, she also facilitated our organizational discipline because she bought into our Vision. She wanted to see us become a world-class company as much as anyone, and she set out to make it happen. If your organization's Vision is an aspirational one—and if it isn't, then it really isn't a Vision—no one person can make it happen. I knew I couldn't handle the CFO role. I've seen too many people who let their ego get in the way in moments like this. They don't, or can't, admit to themselves or others that they need help running the organization, or their ego prevents them from hiring people who are smarter or more knowledgeable than they are.

A good leader has to have an ego, that inner voice that gives them the confidence and drive to take risks and to make something happen. However, you must remember you're the leader. Your job is to make sure the organization is successful, not that you personally get credit for each and every decision. When you're just starting, it's hard sometimes to distinguish between the organization and yourself, because the organization's your baby. But if your organization is to grow, it must become more than a reflection of you. When the organization is successful, you'll get plenty of personal credit, but in the meantime, focus on making the organization itself successful. In our case, we needed an experienced CFO who knew a lot more about financial reporting and tax issues than I did to help Wildcat navigate the growing financial challenges.

The advantage to hiring someone smarter or more knowledgeable than yourself is the additional resources this practice brings to the organization. I leaned on Gina a lot. Frequently, I knew what I wanted to accomplish, but I wasn't sure how to do it or how to do it without creating other issues, such as tax complications. I'd go to Gina's office to lay out an issue and my thoughts, or my partners and I would sit down with her to discuss our plans. She would walk us through the process, advise us on the consequences of taking various options, and frequently raise issues that we hadn't thought of. We would then make an informed decision, and she would help implement that decision.

As helpful as Gina's advice was, it was her fiscal discipline that helped us implement our plans. I've previously described situations where I had to say no to my managers because we had to be so careful and precise with our capital expenditures. There were plenty of times when Gina told me "no." For a leader, there's an important balance between being in charge and having checks in place. How often have you heard a person described as having their biggest strength also be their greatest liability? Maybe you're an outstanding salesperson. If so, your innate belief that you can and should convince someone to buy a product might sometimes override your judgment. A salesperson sees success as closing a deal and, without any outside limits, might sweeten the deal more than they should to close the deal. Similarly, someone who is gifted at reviewing financial statements and controlling costs might fail to recognize a good investment opportunity because they're too focused on cost control.

Gina's ability to say "no" to me and, more importantly, to explain why was priceless. I didn't always like hearing "no"—okay, I never liked hearing "no." I didn't like it because I was excited by the project that we were discussing and I had convinced myself that it was worth the investment. My excitement, however, sometimes prevented me from seeing all the issues. Her analysis provided a check that I needed. If I didn't have a good answer to her objections, it either meant that I hadn't thought the issue through and needed to refine my approach, or that she was right.

As important as her ability to say "no" to me was, her ability and willingness to hold the organization accountable to our Implementation Plan was even more critical. If we decided to spend X dollars, she made sure we spent no more than X and, if possible, we spent less. If our Plan didn't include a particular expenditure, she didn't authorize it. Those refusals caused a lot of frustration among my managers but there was never any doubt in their minds that her heart was in the right place.

Wildcat Oil Tools was my baby. I started it. I made the first sales calls, I delivered the first BOP to the location, I made the decisions to add new pieces of equipment, and so forth and so on. At first, I did it all because I had to. That was fine, because I loved every minute of the process. However, because Wildcat Oil Tools was my baby, I continued wanting to be involved in every aspect of what we did even as we grew. New product lines, locations, and customers fueled this desire because of the excitement for new opportunities. Over time, I realized I could only do so much. If I continued trying to do everything, I'd do it poorly. If I didn't discipline myself, but simply wandered wherever my interests led me, I would potentially neglect more important matters.

It quickly became evident that I could best serve Wildcat Oil Tools by providing structure and guidance through processes and procedures rather than by engaging in micromanagement and by focusing my time in areas of personal strength while allowing others to take over areas where I wasn't as knowledgeable. Gina's hiring is

CHAPTER 9

an excellent example of this strategy, but there were plenty of others. I encourage you to surround yourself with a team that enhances your strengths, addresses your weaknesses, and that is committed to the organization's Vision. Make them responsible for your Vision and Implementation Plan, empower them to do their jobs, and then hold them accountable.

As I close this chapter, I'll leave you with a final thought. Implementation plans are critical to your success and they require a lot of discipline, but that doesn't mean your Plan must be 100 percent complete before you get started, or that it can't be adjusted after you get going. A good Plan will grow and develop along with the organization. A change to the Plan is fine as long as the change is intentional, the revised Plan remains true to your Vision, and the Plan isn't changed simply to solve a short-term problem. At the end of the day, you have to be committed to your Implementation Plan and prepared to address the temptations to depart from it. Consequently, give a lot of thought to your Plan. Make sure it will achieve your Vision, it's workable, and it's something you can commit yourself to with no hesitation, trepidation, or second-guessing.

CHAPTER TEN

GETTING THE RIGHT TEAM

Every successful business that I'm aware of touts their people as their greatest asset, and they're correct to do so. Rarely will any business succeed without talented individuals or survive long if their talent is deficient. Wildcat Oil Tools people are most definitely a key to our success. But that's because we make a constant effort to find, recruit, and retain the right people, to put them in the right positions, and to make sure they've grown with their positions. For a leader, this process is both the best and worst part of the job, because the corollary is that if an individual proves themselves unable or unwilling to meet our expectations, we make a change.

Previously, I discussed the need to surround yourself with a team that complements your personal strengths and weaknesses and is committed to your Vision and Implementation Plan. I gave an example of how I did so with our CFO. Having a team of individuals like our CFO is critical to making you successful as a leader. In this chapter, however, when I refer to our people, I'm including everyone who works for or with Wildcat Oil Tools.

I enjoy recruiting and promoting staff. There's nothing like finding a talented individual, offering them a position or promotion, and seeing the look in their eye when they say "yes." On the other hand, some of the lowest moments of my life have come when I've had to let someone go who, despite their best efforts, wasn't getting the job done. I know of no way to make that process easier and, quite frankly, I'm not sure that you ever want it to be anything other than difficult. But even though these personnel issues are hard, you must make and implement negative personnel decisions in a timely manner or your organization will suffer. If you aren't proactive, difficult personnel decisions will invariably be deferred. For example, when an individual is trying, and it's someone that you've gotten to know and like, it's easy to procrastinate making a difficult decision or having a difficult meeting—I know because I've done both. However, I also know without any doubt that personnel problems which are ignored never solve themselves but will only get worse, and that if you aren't constantly focused on putting the right people in the right positions, you'll never fulfill your organization's potential.

Getting back to the positive. I'm constantly on the lookout for talent, not just to fill a current vacancy, but to improve Wildcat Oil Tools. When a professional sports league, such as the NFL, holds a draft, you see two different philosophies at work: draft for need versus selecting the best player available. When you're running a business, oftentimes you have to fill a need with the best person available. For example, if the CFO retires, it doesn't matter how many talented engineers, salesmen, or information technology (IT) people you see, you hire the individual most capable of taking over the CFO's role even if you aren't completely thrilled with that choice. I've seen

CHAPTER 10

plenty of people run their business by only hiring to fill specific needs. Unquestionably, there is a logic to this process, and when properly administered it helps control costs by preventing you from overstaffing. I hire for need when I must, but my preference is to focus on attracting talent because it frees me to ask the right questions.

When I hire to fill a need, the ultimate question is who is the best person among those that I'm considering? That may mean settling for someone. Go back to the NFL draft. Every NFL team aspires to win the Super Bowl. Super Bowl-winning teams normally have superior quarterbacks. If a team is forced to draft a quarterback one year because their top two quarterbacks retired or signed with other teams, the best one available when it's their turn to make a draft pick may not have the talent or ability necessary to win the Super Bowl. But because the team must draft a quarterback, they're forced to settle for someone with whom they're unlikely to be happy over the long term.

When I'm focused on recruiting talent, I'm free to consider only the people who fit our Vision, and who are committed to that Vision and our Implementation Plan. That allows me to ask, would hiring this person improve our organization and help us achieve our Vision? If the answer is yes, then I have the confidence to explore further. However, if the answer is "no," I can pass on them because I'm not forced to settle for someone. That was particularly important to Wildcat Oil Tools because our Plan required a team-wide commitment to several difficult challenges such as our international expansion.

There are many reasons why most US companies never even consider doing business internationally. For a starter, overseas expansion is risky and complicated. There are innumerable problems that must be considered including taxes, legal and regulatory issues, logistical hurdles, and personnel concerns. You worry about the political developments in every country that you deal with. For example, when the political leadership in a foreign country you're working in changes, you worry about whether the new leaders will change their tax code, import and export procedures, or employment rules, and, if so, how such changes will impact your company. Then, there are the diplomatic issues. If a foreign country that you're working in gets into a dispute with Canada and kicks out the Canadian ambassador, you must immediately ask yourself, "What am I buying in Canada for use in that country and, if necessary, where else can I get it? Do I have any Canadian citizens working for me in that country? If so, do I need to reassign them?"

I knew how important it was to be surrounded by people who wanted to be part of an international expansion, who saw these issues as challenges to be solved, and who were excited about being part of that process. The last thing that I needed was someone in senior management who thought international expansion was a bad idea and should be avoided.

Over the years I learned there truly is no magic formula to determine who the ideal candidate will look like in advance. There were times when I started with an assumption about the ideal candidate, but I quickly learned it was foolish to pre-filter candidates based on any assumption, because it could cost you the opportunity to recruit a superstar. Obviously, some jobs require a certain degree or background. For example, if you need an accountant, you can exclude everyone with no accounting degree and no accounting experience. If you need a general counsel, you look for people with a

CHAPTER 10

law license. What I'm talking about is using as many lines and as few boxes as possible in your employment process.

Take my accountant example. You could easily begin your search by assuming the ideal candidate will have at least X years' experience, will have worked in your industry for a similar company, and will have their Certified Public Accountant certificate. Each of these is a reasonable assumption and none would subject you to any criticism; however they may distract you from finding the most talented individual. In every field, there are a few superstars—that is, individuals who all would agree were, or are, the most talented individuals to ever work in that field. We forget that each one of these individuals started their first job with no prior experience. If they had interviewed with you and your job form had one or more "prior experience" boxes, odds are good that you would have passed on a future superstar because they couldn't check that box.

Prior experience can be, and often is, a huge asset; however, it can also be misleading. I've seen people who list thirty years' experience on their resume. One would assume that this experience created a broad base of knowledge. The reality, however, is that they have one year of experience because for the last twenty-nine years, they've simply repeated what they did their first year. I would much rather hire someone with no experience but a good attitude and a desire to learn, than the person with one year of experience crammed into a thirty-year career.

Don't think I don't value experience. I do. I value good experience. I look for talented people with experiences that make them better fits for Wildcat Oil Tools. Some of our best hires were people with substantial experience who were looking for something different or who had been caught up in a reduction-of-force move at their prior employers. Often these individuals came from a situation that didn't fully take advantage of their talent. Sell them on a Vision, empower them to help you achieve it, and you get an individual whose experience will save you considerable money by avoiding mistakes or who will open doors for you because of their connections.

Formal education is another area where assumptions can get in the way of finding talent. I've seen several individuals who didn't have as much formal education as others in their field but who were incredibly knowledgeable because of their experience. When you dig further into their backgrounds, you'll invariably find they are extremely intelligent, but circumstances beyond their control prevented them from going to college. These people overcame the lack of a college degree with hard work, a quest for knowledge, and self-discipline. I'll always take that individual over a college graduate who, because of their family circumstances, had a guaranteed education at a highly-regarded university given to them and has never needed to work for anything. I know the individual who attended the school of hard knocks has the will to overcome challenges because they have; I don't know what to expect when the college graduate encounters their first significant obstacle or challenge.

In fact, when hiring, I look for individuals who have overcome hardship. It doesn't matter what the hardship was; give me a group of people who were dealt a serious blow and could have given up but didn't, choosing instead to work harder than their peers to overcome the challenge, and I'll take on the world. Those individuals have a strength of character that I never worry about because they didn't give up when they easily and understandably could have. Because they didn't give up then, they're highly unlikely to give up when faced with a new challenge at Wildcat Oil Tools.

Assembling the right team also includes finding good fits and avoiding mismatches. Every company has a culture, and different facilities or departments within a large company will have slightly different cultures. You want candidates who are good cultural fits for your organization. That can mean saying "no" to qualified people. When we opened a technology center in Houston to work on our proprietary tools, we needed someone with a strong background in engineering and quality control to oversee this facility. Quality control is critical for any company but was particularly important for Wildcat's new tools. When you introduce a new tool in the marketplace, you truly have one chance to make a first impression. A new tool must absolutely, positively, and without exception, work correctly and perform as advertised both during field trials and for your customers. A company with a long track record of successfully developing new tools can overcome a failure with enough time and capital. Because we were just starting our research and development department, we didn't have that luxury. Our new tools had to work correctly the first time. Consequently, the technology center was crucial to our ability to develop and market new tools.

We visited with several candidates to oversee this center, and we found people with good experience and educational backgrounds. Unfortunately, we didn't find one who was a good fit. The technology center director works closely with the entire research and development team. Oftentimes they collaborate under stressful conditions. We needed someone who could handle the stress, who was attentive to detail, and who would work well with the other members of the research and development team. I was concerned the people I had interviewed couldn't do so. It wasn't because they were unqualified or didn't work hard; rather, my concern was about their ability to work with the research and development team. A personality dispute in that setting would seriously undermine our efforts and at that stage in our development, I couldn't take the risk.

We ultimately decided to promote James Bradley, a young engineer who was already working for us. James had interned with Wildcat Oil Tools while he was in college and came to work for us full-time after graduation. At the time, he had been with the company for two years. James didn't have nearly as much experience as the other people we visited with, but I knew he was talented, and he worked well with our research and development team in stressful situations. We worked around his lack of experience by giving him access to outside resources. I'm pleased to say James has excelled in his new position and has grown as an engineer. Equally important, Wildcat Oil Tools is a better company today than if I had hired someone who, while more experienced, wasn't a fit.

I appreciate that some will say a cultural fit test is a handy way to hide discriminatory hiring practices. Personally, I don't have to worry about that. Even a cursory examination of our ownership, top management, and staff will quickly reveal we are a diverse company. Discrimination is a product of intent. If your intent is to exclude a group, then I suppose you could try to cover yourself by explaining you didn't hire someone because you felt they weren't a fit and it's simply coincidental that this person was a member of a particular group and that members of that group are never deemed good fits. If so, that's your loss. The talent that you're excluding will

CHAPTER 10

find a job with your competition and if you let your competitors assemble more talent than you have, that imbalance will eventually be reflected in both your books and in theirs. In the meantime, I'm going to continue assembling teams of talented people who will make Wildcat Oil Tools more successful. Finding people who are good fits for our culture is an important part of this process.

Attitude is also important when recruiting. I've heard it said you should hire for attitude and train for skills, and in my experience, that advice is spot-on. I can take someone with a good attitude and teach them the skills they need to know, but I can't fix a bad attitude. Worse, a bad attitude not only affects the individual, it acts like a cancer and negatively impacts the other members of their team.

Making Wildcat Oil Tools the world's premier fishing and tool company required people who were comfortable with risks and challenges and who were flexible thinkers. When we started expanding Wildcat Oil Tools from one location to several across the country, when we added a research and development department, when we added new product lines, and when we expanded internationally, we necessarily encountered unexpected problems and roadblocks. Before each expansion, we knew some of the challenges that we'd have to face, but we also knew unexpected problems would come our way. There are legions of individuals who are outstanding employees and wonderful people who would not be happy facing this uncertainty. Thus, when I say a person didn't have the right attitude, I'm not being critical. If I were putting together a soccer team, I'd look for soccer players, not basketball players—not because basketball players are bad athletes, but because they aren't what I need. In my case, I needed people who were motivated by the prospect of building an international company; I didn't need people who would get anxious and would share their anxiety with others.

Consequently, I spent a lot of time with potential employees discussing my Vision to gauge their reactions. During interviews, I asked the normal job-related questions, but I also encouraged people to simply talk. What they said was important. Equally important was how they said it. Were they excited about the Vision? Would I want to spend time with them? Could I trust them with Wildcat Oil Tools' brand? Did they strike me as someone willing to learn, to take risks, and to do new things? If we were in the middle of a crisis, would I feel good knowing that they were there with me? Because I focus more on finding talent than filling needs, I had the freedom to not hire people who were, at least on paper, qualified but whose response to my Vision didn't register.

Building the right team doesn't end with recruiting. You must continuously focus on having the right people in the right positions. People and organizations are rarely stagnant. That means occasionally changing people's roles because their job responsibilities outgrow their abilities. Unfortunately, it can also mean parting ways with an individual. Letting someone go or transferring them to a less desirable position is never easy, but you'll never fulfill your organization's potential if you neglect these decisions. I once received a great piece of advice: if I were interviewing one of my employees for their current job, would I hire them again? If the answer is "no," then it's time to make a change.

Like everyone else, we sometimes hired people who didn't perform up to the level we had expected, and we had people who, because of personal situations, experienced a decline in their work performance. In those instances, we had to part ways. We also had people who couldn't keep up with our growth. When we were a small company with one location, a handful of products and employees, and a few customers, everyone wore multiple hats. When a person is in this role, they don't necessarily have to be an expert on any one task. However, as we grew, our roles became more focused and required more sophistication.

For example, overseeing the sales department when it consisted of two salesmen working at one location and selling a few standard rental tools was a much different job than overseeing salesmen at multiple locations across the US. That job changed again when international sales was added. Another change occurred when we started selling our own proprietary tools because we had to convince our customers to use a newly-designed tool on a well that cost several million dollars to drill. A person who could do a phenomenal job overseeing the sales department in the beginning couldn't necessarily handle the sales department as it evolved.

I use the sales position as an example because our vice president of operations, Alfred Fuentes, is a terrific example of someone growing with the job. The more we expanded, the better he became. He started as a salesman, became a sales manager, then the head of our sales department, and today is responsible for our operations division. Others, unfortunately, couldn't match our growth and we were forced to make a change. Terminating or reassigning someone you've outgrown is difficult. First, because the job's evolution is gradual, it's not always clear when an individual becomes misplaced. Second, there's the human factor. If you catch someone stealing, making a change is easy because morally they deserved their fate.

However, when they could do the job they were originally hired to do, but can't do the job that it's evolved into, the change doesn't feel fair. When an individual isn't capable of keeping up, however, they're holding the organization back.

Fortunately, you normally have some options in this instance. For example, if I have someone who is otherwise an asset, I try to put them in a position where they can succeed. It will feel like a demotion because, quite frankly, it normally is; but after they've had a chance to get over the disappointment, they're usually happier in a revised role. There may be some initial denial, but most people come to recognize they weren't performing fully. If they can be convinced they are still valued members of the team, and they experience success in their revised roles, they'll become assets.

A related question is, what happens when you find someone that's better than the person you currently have? There's no bright-line answer. If you want your people to be loyal to the organization, then you must be loyal to them. If you start making changes that appear to be based on a flavor-of-the-month analysis, your people will feel insecure and their performance will suffer. Consequently, if the person you currently have is meeting expectations, I wouldn't make a change. On the other hand, if they're holding you back, then it may be time to consider a change. Use the "Would I hire this person again?" test. If the answer is that you wouldn't hire them, period, then it's clearly time to make a change. If the answer is that you would hire them, but not for this position, then consider a reassignment or restructuring.

In Wildcat's case, our growth changed the nature of several positions. I've mentioned the changes to oversight of the sales department. Every other area of the company encountered a similar situation. That growth allowed me to bring on new people who were better qualified to take on the new challenge and to reassign current employees to roles that better fit their talents.

Our growth also required me to be cognizant, not only of our current needs, but of our expected future needs. For example, before we opened our research and development department, I knew we would need people capable of designing new tools and getting them patented. I started asking friends and contacts if they knew of anyone who could fill these roles and would be a good fit. I kept my ears open and talked to potential candidates. Because I was proactive, I had the luxury of taking as much time as I needed to find the right people. I had many other things going on, and it would have been easy to procrastinate, but had I waited until we absolutely had to have someone, it could have led to us taking someone we weren't excited about.

At the end of the day, keep in mind, although it's your team, the organization will only go as far as they will take it. Close enough is never good enough and good today doesn't guarantee success tomorrow. Assure yourself continually that you have the right person in the right place and keep your eyes open for talent. Finally, never put off the difficult personnel issues. The quicker you take care of these, the better off you and the people involved will be.

CHAPTER ELEVEN

COMMUNICATION

It goes without saying that good leaders are good communicators. It's impossible to lead a group if people don't understand and appreciate what you're trying to accomplish. When you think of the most successful leaders in history, you'll probably immediately recall a famous speech or presentation that they gave. For example, remember Lincoln's Gettysburg Address, Steve Jobs's new product announcements, and Martin Luther King's "I Have a Dream" speech. Each of these moments was defining, memorable, and critical to each person's ultimate success. Even though we remember them for what they said, however, I'm willing to bet that President Lincoln, Steve Jobs, and Dr. King were also excellent listeners. In my experience, the ability and willingness to listen is crucial to a leader's ability to communicate and, therefore, to their success.

Listening was a key part of my early managerial growth. I attribute much of what I know as a leader to my mentors and my desire to learn from them. I've also learned a lot from the people whom I've supervised. I worked at Blockbuster, Sears, and Nabors before starting Wildcat Oil Tools. During that time, I frequently managed people who were older than I was. I made it a point to seek their advice and I then incorporated what I learned from them into my decision making. Experience is often a lesson learned from a mistake. If I could learn from my older supervisees' mistakes and, therefore, avoiding making similar errors, I was ahead of the game. Learning from their victories was equally valuable because I had examples of successful strategies. Finally, listening to these supervisees was important because they felt valued and, thus, they were more likely to step in and prevent me from doing something stupid in the future.

I was fortunate to have a strong mentor during my first management position with Nabors. This position required me to participate in budget discussions, business growth strategy meetings, and financial evaluations. During these meetings, I focused on listening and learning. I knew my knowledge was limited and I could only learn if I kept my mouth shut and my ears open, so I asked questions before or after the meeting if I had any concerns. I made it a point to keep notes because it helped me pay attention and I retained more.

At times, I was asked to express an opinion. This request can be scary for a new executive because you risk embarrassment. However, I knew if I couldn't or wouldn't express an opinion when asked, they would find someone else who would. I developed a strategy to handle the fear. When I was asked for an opinion, I wouldn't offer a bare opinion, I set out my analysis, and I did so with as much confidence as I could muster. I learned the group was more interested in my analysis and reasoning than my opinion, because a person with good

CHAPTER 11

analytical skills can be trained to make better judgments. That lesson stuck with me, and I'll refer to it later as a way to improve your team's performance.

Listening is key to good leadership for two reasons: what you hear increases your knowledge; furthermore, when the leadership listens, the organization develops. As the old saying goes, "God gave us two ears and one mouth for a reason." You'll never fully understand what is going on in your organization, and why, unless you're a good listener and you encourage your managers and supervisors to be good listeners. This commitment requires that you make people feel comfortable coming to you with bad news as well as for support, guidance, and motivation.

You learn a lot about your organization when you listen to people at all levels. Some of the best ideas that Wildcat Oil Tools has ever had came from unlikely sources and at unlikely times. We also avoided mistakes by listening when one of our field staff members said, "You know, if you do that . . ." If I hadn't put myself in a position to hear those ideas and warnings, or I hadn't been listening, I would have missed them. If our organization's culture had discouraged people from speaking up, our performance would have suffered. I've also learned a lot about what was going on not only by listening to what people said, but also noticing how they said it, and, sometimes, realizing what they hadn't said. In today's busy world, where text messages are replacing personal conversations, it's becoming increasingly easy to miss these nonverbal cues. Don't allow this to happen to you.

This topic brings up a challenge that Wildcat's growth created. Today, the hardest part of listening to people throughout the organization is physically putting myself in a position where I can do this listening. When we started with a single location, I knew everyone's names, the names of their spouses and children, and what they liked to do after work. I also knew their personal work habits and behaviors. Consequently, it wasn't hard to notice when something wasn't right and, therefore, I knew I needed to learn if there was a work-related issue. One disadvantage of our growth is that I no longer know everyone that well, and I can't always spot the signs that something isn't right. They say "ignorance is bliss." That adage may be true in some circumstances, but not when it prevents you from appreciating a problem exists before it becomes a major issue.

Geography has also played a role in our communication challenges. When we had one location, I saw everyone regularly. Now that we have yards across the nation and operations internationally, I simply can't see everyone. I do my best to get to all our locations, but unfortunately, my schedule limits my time in one spot, and I normally have a list of things that must be accomplished before I leave. Consequently, I don't have the time that I would like to shoot the bull and chat with employees about their families.

Another disadvantage to our growth is that I don't know as much about the company's day-to-day activities as I did when we first started. In the beginning, when I was driving the trailer with our equipment to the location, I knew every customer representative, what every customer was renting, how well our equipment had performed, and if there were any problems. Today, although I get out in the field whenever possible, I spend much more of my time in the office working with my partners and our senior management team, or in my customers' offices meeting with their CEOs and senior staff members. I keep up to date with daily written operational reports, but this information is relatively sterile. The reports don't give me the same feel that I had when I was delivering our equipment to the customer's location.

To overcome these disadvantages, I make it an absolute priority to go to each of our yards and offices personally on a regular basis. The travel takes a toll and it's sometimes tempting to try to handle everything on the phone, but unless I get out and about, I miss a lot. When I go to a yard or office, I not only visit with the manager and supervisors, I walk through the facility and personally speak with as many employees as possible. Even if I only shake hands and say "hello," people appreciate the effort. These walk-throughs also give me a chance to see for myself how things are going and to observe morale.

You can tell a lot through a person's body language. Phone calls, video conferences, emails, text messages, and social media posts are terrific ways to communicate information, but how a person says something is frequently more important than what they said. You don't get that information, especially from your frontline people, unless you get out on the frontline and make those people comfortable enough to speak up. You accomplish this task by drawing them out. Shake their hands, look them in their eyes, and have fun. You might have to give someone a hard time, or make yourself the butt of the joke, but be sure to get past the "How's it going?" and "Fine" conversation. The key is to convince everyone that you care about them and that you want to hear what they have to say. So, when they do start talking, listen. Forget your phone, your watch, and your schedule. Give them enough time to speak, ask questions, and thank them for the information. If at all possible, follow up later to demonstrate you were listening and do care. You may have to say "no" to a request or suggestion, but the morale boost they get for being appreciated will far offset the disappointment they feel because of the negative news.

Personal visits like these are good for morale, but they can't be the organization's only effort to listen. In my case, I have to rely on my facility managers to listen to their employees and to communicate that information to me. I make it clear to my managers that I expect them to have good lines of communication with their employees. I reinforce that expectation during my personal visits by asking questions such as, "What do the operators think?" I can tell from their responses how informed they are about their employees' moods. If I ever detect a manager isn't listening, I hold that manager accountable. Fortunately, this unwillingness to listen is rarely an issue because I've got several outstanding managers; however, it never hurts to remind them how important good communication is to me.

Listening can be difficult when you're pressed for time. When I do not have time for someone, I try to explain why I can't speak now, and then assure them that I want to hear what they have to say. If possible, I suggest a better time. Otherwise, I do my dead-level best to follow-up later.

Listening is also difficult when you're getting bad news. Ask any CEO their views on receiving bad news and you'll hear them say you shouldn't shoot the messenger. In the abstract, this is a no-brainer piece of advice. In the real world, putting that advice into practice can be difficult to follow. Imagine someone is admitting a mistake, is criticizing your idea, or is telling you that things aren't going as expected. In the abstract, we would all agree these are things that the CEO doesn't want to hear but needs to know. In the real world, however, some CEOs don't get this information in a timely manner because their employees are afraid to deliver bad news.

Imagine you're the CEO and you've just received bad news. Your immediate reaction to the messenger will determine how others will act in the future. If you take your anger or frustration out on the messenger, you can expect a lot of avoidance behavior from your people in the future. Obviously, an angry reaction's not healthy for the organization, but it's also an easy mistake to make because of the emotions involved. Here are my suggestions for handling three common bad news situations.

In the first situation, someone comes to you and admits they've made a mistake. To be clear, I'm not suggesting you give anyone a free pass for their mistakes. In fact, if you want your organization to succeed, you have to hold people accountable. However, if there's no difference between the way you treat the person who owns up to a mistake and the person who fails to say anything, you can expect more coverups and fewer disclosures in the future. When someone makes a mistake, particularly a serious one, their first instinct will be to cover it up. If you don't believe me, wait till you make your next big mistake and see what thoughts immediately pop into your head. You want your organization's culture to counter-balance this instinct. It's been my experience that bad news doesn't get better with time. A delay in reporting, therefore, will most likely make the problem even worse which, in turn, further incentivizes the individual to hide the problem. Ultimately, individuals decide whether to cover up their mistakes and they should be held accountable for those decisions, but anything you can do to encourage someone to come forward when they've made a mistake will further the organization's success.

How you encourage openness will vary greatly depending on the circumstances, but the key is that everyone in the organization should appreciate that while you will forgive mistakes, you will always deal harshly with anyone who attempts to cover one up. I've made my fair share of mistakes and I've learned a lot from them. My goal is never to make the same mistake twice. I do all that I can to promote the same for Wildcat Oil Tools as an organization. I do that, in part, by focusing everyone on forward thinking.

We put considerable emphasis on learning, as an organization, from the mistakes that individuals make. To promote learning, when we have an incident, we must understand what happened, why, and how the same mistake can be avoided in the future. As part of our fact-finding, we interview the people who were involved. I need them to be truthful and forthcoming. So, when I meet with the individual who made the mistake, I don't yell, curse, or otherwise demean them. Instead, I walk them through what happened and why, and we discuss ways to avoid making the same mistake in the future. In addition to learning the facts, I want to focus on the individual's thought processes during our discussion. If their thought process during the incident was faulty, fixing it will prevent a wide range of other incidents in the future. If their thought process was good but the execution faulty, then we concentrate on job processes. In either event, focusing them on solutions, rather than on immediate personal consequence, encourages full disclosure of the information that I need to know.

CHAPTER 11

We take this information and use it as a teaching tool for the entire organization by explaining what happened and why, and how similar incidents can be avoided in the future. When we do so, we avoid demeaning the individual or individuals involved. Generally, everyone knows who was involved and if any disciplinary action was taken. I want our folks to stop focusing on the company's punitive response, if any, and to start focusing on how to avoid the same mistake. So, when we describe an incident, we don't say, "John was a real idiot." We set out the facts objectively and then we immediately move on to solutions. The ensuing discussion focuses solely on the solution. I hope that by using these actions, our culture encourages self-reporting and learning.

In the second situation, someone criticizes your idea. I'm an idea person. Like every other idea person, I've had a combination of good and bad ideas. Fortunately, we've implemented more of my good ideas than my bad ideas and almost all the bad ideas died on the vine before we did anything; every now and then, however, a bad idea slips through. If we're doing something that is causing problems or is having unintended consequence in the field, I need to know about it now. Because I don't get to spend as much time in the field as I would like, I usually need someone to tell me we've got a problem. It's never fun to listen to someone when they tell you that one of your ideas isn't working or shouldn't be adopted, because it feels like they're criticizing you. The question is, would you rather have people inflate your ego or help the organization reach its potential? Find a way to hear someone criticize your idea without taking it personally.

To encourage people to disclose their mistakes and to let me know when one of my ideas isn't a good one, I do my best to lead by example. When I make a mistake, I own up to it. I don't blame anyone else or otherwise try to deflect the blame. When it's clear that we're doing something incorrectly or taking an action that has unintended consequence, I'll take personal credit for the bad idea even if it wasn't entirely mine. In both instances, I've found that a little self-deprecating humor helps. Then, I immediately focus the group on solutions. I want people to realize mistakes happen and when they do, we aren't going to waste time crucifying someone or looking for a scapegoat. Instead, we're going to identify the issue, determine a corrective action, and then implement the action. We still hold people accountable, but I do that privately. The only person to get criticized publicly is me.

In the third situation, things aren't going as well as expected. Maybe the sales numbers are low, the expense numbers are high, or a new product isn't competitive. Imagine you're the one who's drawn the black bean and gets to deliver the bad news to the boss. If you know you're going to be yelled at, regardless of fault, you'll delay the meeting as long as possible and then when you do deliver the news, you'll sugarcoat it. Now, put your boss hat back on and imagine that someone approached you that way. What are the odds that the problem will have solved itself during the delay? How likely is your initial response to be adequate if you weren't given all the details? In both cases, the answer is probably nil.

There are only two ways to avoid this outcome. First, you must commit yourself to not venting when someone delivers bad news. That doesn't mean you won't get angry. I do. In fact, I've never been able to prevent myself from experiencing an emotion. I do, however, have complete control over my actions. When I play golf, I get as

CHAPTER 11

angry at myself as anyone else after a bad shot, but long ago I decided I wasn't going to throw a club—so I don't. The same holds true when people deliver bad news. Because you've previously decided not to vent on the messenger, you can focus on the message. Listen, ask questions, and make sure you fully understand the situation or at least know what's known and unknown. Finally, make sure to thank the messenger before they leave. People are more apt to tell you what you need to hear if they feel appreciated for having done so.

You can also discourage delayed reporting and sugarcoating by holding people accountable when they do so. I want people to understand no one will ever be punished for breaking bad news, but anyone caught lying or hiding information will be. It takes a certain amount of trust and self-confidence for someone to tell you what you need to know instead of what you want to hear. You promote that trust when your people know they won't be criticized simply for delivering bad news.

This topic leads to a related discussion. How do you get people to talk? I've discussed specific methods of dealing with avoidance behavior. But what about the situation where an individual lacks the confidence to speak up at meetings? If you'll recall, when I started attending management meetings at Nabors, I was sometimes asked for an opinion. I eventually learned they asked because they wanted to know more about my thought process than to learn what my opinion was. I've carried that lesson with me to Wildcat Oil Tools.

Sometimes I just need to know an answer. For example, if I have a legal question, I ask my general counsel what the law is on a particular issue. I don't want to know how he analyzed the statute or case law to give me an answer, I just want to know what the law is.

It's the "Tell me what time it is and not how to make a watch" adage. When I've got a new manager or supervisor, however, I'm generally more interested in how they got to their decision than I am in the decision itself. That new manager or supervisor may have some of the same concerns about speaking up that I had at Nabors when I was asked for my opinion at a managers' meeting. If so, that's fine as long as they can overcome their hesitation and speak up, because I need to know if they can make a decision and, if so, how did they analyze the problem?

Here's a trick: when you have a group of managers assembled for a meeting, make the newest manager offer an opinion before they hear anyone else's. My friends with military experience tell me that when a group of officers is discussing an issue, they'll frequently make the lowest-ranking officer go first. That way he or she has no idea what their boss is thinking, and they can't shade their opinion. At Wildcat Oil Tools, I like to follow a similar approach. In a group session, I'll frequently ask the junior manager for an opinion before I ask their boss. If it's just me and my manager, I'll ask them for their opinion before I offer any analysis so that they can't simply agree with me. I'll politely push back if they try to defer, but I won't insist on a response because I have to know if they're willing to make a decision. If they can't offer me an opinion in this situation, then I'm making a change.

After I hear their opinion, I'll ask some probing questions to see how they analyzed the issue. As I've said before, I need to know their thought processes in order to evaluate their performances fully. I can live with rookie mistakes as long as the staff members who make them are actively thinking. Asking these types of questions has the added benefit of making the employee feel valued. If I didn't care about them, I wouldn't bother to ask why they were making a particular recommendation. By walking them through the issue, however, I demonstrate that I do, in fact, care about them and value their contribution.

Sometimes the individual offers an ill-informed opinion because of their lack of experience. When this happens, I use it as a positive learning moment and not a personal beat-down opportunity. You won't hear me tell a new manager or supervisor, "That's a stupid idea." What you will hear me say is their idea won't work because of X and I explain why. I compliment where appropriate and otherwise reinforce the notion that they shouldn't be afraid to speak up.

I'll end this chapter with some practical steps that you can take that will make you a better listener. First, put away the phone, computer, and any other distraction when you're talking to someone. Listen to understand, not to reply. You can think faster than someone can talk, so it's normal for you to start thinking about what you'll say when they stop talking. Resist that urge and put yourself in their shoes to make sure you fully understand what they're saying. Ask a follow-up question. Take notes. Look at the speaker. At the end, summarize what you've heard to make sure they agree.

CHAPTER TWELVE
RESPONDING TO ADVERSITY

Every organization faces adversity, whether it's cash flow, personnel problems, or bad publicity from an unhappy customer. Because these problems are expected, their appearance is usually not the source of a crisis atmosphere within the organization. In addition, every business also has unexpected problems. In extreme cases, these problems can threaten the viability of the organization. I've often heard it said that adversity doesn't develop character; instead, it reveals character. In my experience, that's definitely true for businesses, because the organization's response will reveal its priorities as well as its strengths and weaknesses.

That includes the strengths and weakness of its leaders. Effective leaders don't let themselves or the organization become fixated with the problem; rather, they move to solutions. A great example of this was Admiral Chester Nimitz immediately after Pearl Harbor. In the aftermath of the December 7th attack, he was asked to take over command of the American Pacific fleet. He arrived at Pearl Harbor on Christmas Eve and was given a tour of the harbor.

He saw the tremendous destruction wrought by the Japanese military's surprise attack. Sunken battleships and naval vessels were scattered throughout the harbor. Numerous buildings had been destroyed and several soldiers and sailors had been killed or wounded. Nimitz noticed a spirit of despair, dejection, and defeat wherever he looked. To any observer, the situation would have appeared hopeless. Nimitz, however, saw things differently.

Immediately after the tour, he surprised people by not commenting on the destruction, but by stating the Japanese had made three of the biggest mistakes that an attacking force could make. First, they attacked on Sunday, when nine out of ten sailors were on leave. Had they attacked on any other day of the week the casualties would have been 38,000 instead of 3,800. Second, the Japanese were so focused on attacking battleships that they never once bombed the harbor's dry docks. Consequently, the damaged ships could be raised, taken to a local dry dock by a tug for repair, and be ready to return to service in less time than it would have taken simply to haul them to the mainland. Third, every drop of fuel the Americans had in the Pacific theater was still in storage tanks located on the surface, five miles away. One plane could have destroyed all of these tanks and left the Americans without any fuel, but the Japanese failed to do so.

Nimitz's observations help shift people's attention from the widespread destruction to the fact that the Pacific fleet had the resources at Pearl Harbor to repair their ships quickly, and also had plenty of sailors and fuel available to then get them back into the war. I imagine the Americans stationed in Hawaii were desperate to get into the fight but, because of their preoccupation with the problems, they didn't realize their opportunities to do so. I'm sure they were operating on the assumption that they were helpless until reinforcements arrived from the mainland. I also imagine as soon as people realized solutions were immediately available, they stopped feeling sorry for themselves and began attacking the problems with a vengeance.

As a leader, you can and should do the same for your organization. Later in this chapter, I'll talk about unrealistic optimism and the need for honest assessments of your problems. For now, though, my point is you can't allow your organization to become so fixated with the problem that they fail to consider solutions. Just as Admiral Nimitz got people to snap out of their depression over the fact that the fleet was at the bottom of the harbor and to start working on getting those ships to dry dock, you must shift your organization's thinking from "Woe for us" to "Okay, this stinks, but we can…." Even if the initial proposals are rejected, at least your people are focusing their energy in a positive direction and that thought process will ultimately lead to a plan of action.

You do model positive thinking by setting an example and by controlling the agenda. When adversity strikes, don't allow your people to see any sign of panic—even if that's what you're secretly feeling. Panic is contagious. Your tone, your mannerisms, and even the way you walk should convey the message, "We've got this." Wishful thinking won't make the problem go away, but if you can convince your people that the problem will be solved, you can ease their anxiety and get them to focus on solutions.

Identify the problem, but as quickly as you can, steer the conversation to solutions. I assume as soon as Admiral Nimitz pointed out that Pear Harbor's dry docks were undamaged, people stopped worrying about things they couldn't control and started working on getting damaged ships to those dry docks. Do the same for your organization. Don't let people spend an inordinate amount of time discussing what you don't have, can't do, or what could happen if the problem isn't solved; get them focused on the resources and opportunities that you do have. Even if the initial suggestions are bad, I'd rather have people focused on a bad solution than feeling sorry for themselves. We can improve a bad idea, but a defeatist attitude is hard to overcome.

An organization's leadership is critical when adversity hits, but your organization's culture may be even more important when determining whether you'll survive and what you'll look like if you do. For example, if you repeatedly tell everyone how important your people are, but at the first sign of trouble you display a shallow disregard for them, your organization's culture will soon reflect a lack of trust and loyalty. In that instance, when adversity hits, I don't care how well you project confidence or how well you focus internal discussion. Your people may say the right things to you, but they'll be spending most of their energy worrying about themselves and their future and they'll be quick to jump ship if an opportunity presents itself. On the other hand, if your people believe and trust you, and they feel valued by the organization, they're invested in the organization's success. These people aren't spending time and energy looking for another job, they're looking for solutions. They aren't gossiping with their co-workers, they're brainstorming ideas. It doesn't take much imagination to see how much more successful the second organization will be at finding a solution than the first one. It also doesn't take much imagination to see how the second organization will come out even stronger, because when a group of people who are committed to one another successfully overcomes adversity together, they develop tighter bonds.

The bottom line, then, is that your organization's culture is critical to your ability to overcome the inevitable adversity. Therefore, you should make it a priority to determine what the ideal culture will look like and how you'll achieve it. When you do so, first consider your Vision. Success requires a strong connection between your organization's culture and your Vision. Each one should support the other. If they don't, your chances of fulfilling your Vision are slim. You've seen how much, at Wildcat Oil Tools, we stressed looking and acting like a world-class company from the beginning even though by any normal measurement we were a small, locally owned and operated service provider. The image that Wildcat Oil Tools projected became the foundation of our culture. We reinforced this image when faced with adversity by always remaining true to our Vision and Implementation Plan, particularly when it was difficult to do so.

Second, take off the rose-colored glasses and honestly determine what your culture is now. This process isn't easy. You're busy, it's hard to grade yourself honestly, and your employees may be reluctant to say something negative to you. So, if you need outside help to get a correct read on your culture, go get it. If you learn your culture isn't consistent with your Vision, then fix it. This step is where you have to be completely committed to your Vision and you have to have good information, because you may learn the problem with your culture is you.

Learning that you're the problem will either be one of the best things that ever happened to you—or one of the worst. It's up to you and your ego. If you're committed to the Vision, your ego won't prevent you from making the changes that you need to make, no matter how difficult or painful the process, and you'll be a better person for having undergone that process. If you're not committed to the Vision, you won't be committed to the solution and things will never truly change. In that case, you should reconsider your Vision.

Let's assume your culture isn't perfect, but it's healthy, it's consistent with your Vision, and you're tweaking things to improve it. Things are rocking along normally until one day when you encounter significant adversity. Your response will either further your Vision or gut it. In Wildcat's case, for example, our research and development department created a cashflow problem. To create a research and development department from scratch meant that we had to make a significant investment in people, facilities, and equipment. We did so with no guarantee that we would ever develop marketable new technology. Intuitively, we understood there would be a period of time during which the research and development department was all cost but no income. We were, however, optimistic. We had good people, a terrific product idea, and a solid marketing plan. Thus, it was easy for us to tell ourselves that this department was an investment that would soon pay for itself. Then reality hit. Everything cost more and took longer than we had anticipated—a lot more and considerably longer.

In the short-term, the cashflow problem had to be addressed. We had several options. One was to cut back or eliminate our research and development department. That choice, however, would have been inconsistent with our Vision of making Wildcat Oil Tools the premier fishing and tool rental company in the world. Instead, we found other ways to meet our cashflow needs while still providing our research and development department the opportunity to develop new tools and our sales department the resources necessary to market those tools. Doing anything else would have been perceived internally as admitting failure and that simply wasn't an option. We didn't always know how we would do it, but we always knew we would ultimately have a profitable research and development effort.

The cashflow crunch forced us to reevaluate Wildcat Oil Tools' Vision. Did we take the easy solution even though it compromised that Vision? Or, did we recommit to the Vision and implement a more difficult solution? When you have similar problems, you'll necessarily consider your Vision and Implementation Plan as you look for a solution. Thus, if you change your Plan or Vision, this change, at least, will be intentional. Believe it or not, it's the day-to-day problem-solving that will better test your Vision commitment and it'll happen without you even realizing it.

By their nature, the day-to-day problems that every organization encounters are distracting. There's a strong incentive to solve the day's problem quickly and efficiently so that you can get back to your normal operations sooner. Make no mistake, efficient problem-solving is a worthwhile endeavor. You cannot, however, allow your problems to prevent you secretly from achieving your Vision or from sticking to your Implementation Plan. Thoughts such as, "Just this once," or "Let's get past this situation," or "We'll do it differently in the future," can easily and unwittingly lead you to create new habits and methods of operation that are inconsistent with your Implementation Plan, but which will become the norm.

It's easy to think of your Vision as a big-picture item and your daily problems as smaller issues. While the organization's Vision is a big-picture item, your Implementation Plan consists of innumerable small processes and actions. If your Vision is a worthwhile one, the Implementation Plan will require a sustained commitment. If not, then perhaps you should reconsider the Vision because you want a Vision that sets your organization apart. If the Implementation Plan is easy, odds are that your organization is average at best.

Nonetheless, when you're working on the latest problem-caused distraction, you can easily find yourself tempted to depart from the Implementation Plan by taking a shortcut. Recall my earlier discussion about the temptation to purchase salvaged pumps rather than new ones. Even though you tell yourself that this is a "Just this once" solution, if you ever allow yourself to take one step on this path, you can easily look up one day and realize the "Just this once" shortcuts are now the company SOP and have supplanted your Implementation Plan. On the other hand, when you remain committed to the implementation despite adversity, you automatically reinforce your Vision. This is one of the reasons why I put considerably more emphasis on Wildcat's Implementation Plan than I did on our Vision.

Before I explain how that worked at Wildcat Oil Tools, let's go back to my steakhouse example from Chapter Two. Imagine your Vision is to serve the best steak in your town and to have service and an atmosphere consistent with that product. You've determined what type of culture you need to achieve this Vision and, while not perfect, your culture is consistent with the Vision and you've

CHAPTER 12

identified the things that you want to do both personally and for the organization to improve it. Then, one day a fire breaks out in the kitchen and much of your cooking equipment is damaged. To make matters worse, your insurance agent warns you that your damages may not be fully covered. The kitchen must be fixed or you're out of business, so you sit down with your accountant to review the books.

During your meeting, the accountant suggests cutting expenses by purchasing lower-quality meat. Because your monthly meat bill is one of your largest expenses and, unlike your rent, is subject to some control, compromising on quality is a tempting option. You know if you purchase lower-quality meat, however, you can't serve the best steak in town. Nonetheless, you could easily rationalize this by saying to yourself, "Our cashflow problems are due to a temporary issue and as soon as I get past this, I'll start buying better-quality meat again; and besides, it's better to cut this cost than to consider laying one of my staff members off."

To be sure, if you're running a restaurant, controlling food costs is critical, so no one would ever castigate you for saving money on your meat purchases. On the other hand, you can't serve the best steak in town without buying top-quality meat and, in fact, a key component of your Implementation Plan is using nothing but top-quality meat and produce. In the moment, situations like this can feel like one-offs, but the reality is cashflow problems have a bad habit of reoccurring. Thus, in this instance you'd have to ask yourself, "When problems like this arise, will I pursue my Vision or not?"

Ultimately, your situation may be such that you only have two realistic choices: purchase lower-quality meat or close your doors. If so, do what you must do today, and you worry about the fallout later.

On the other hand, if you make it clear that serving anything less than the best steak in town is unacceptable and you keep pushing, you may find there are other solutions. People have a habit of falling into comfort zones. I know I do. When that happens, I have to push myself to get back in gear because all too often my limits are self-imposed. I'm capable of doing a lot more than I'll allow myself to consider when I'm too comfortable. As a leader, you sometimes must push your organization out of its collective comfort zone.

In my steakhouse example, pushing people to think past the easy solution to find one that may be more difficult, but which is consistent with your Vision and Implementation Plan, is an opportunity to cement that Vision and Plan. A fire is a major event, but you're going to encounter unexpected expenses with an unhappy regularity. Solving the cashflow problem by buying lower-quality meat is an easy solution because it probably requires no more than a phone call to your supplier. Anything else is likely to be difficult. However, if you sacrifice your Vision or Implementation Plan to solve a short-term problem, you can't expect anyone—yourself included—to remain committed to the Vision and Implementation Plan when other problems arise. However, if you make it crystal clear to your organization that you're committed to the Vision and Plan, you can expect to see your people approach problem-solving with this in mind.

I'm sure Henry Ford confronted several instances where there was an easy answer to a problem, but that answer was inconsistent with his goal of producing a well-made car that the masses could afford. One of the reasons why we remember Ford, and not his contemporaries, is that he didn't take the easy way out; instead, he did things that no one else had been able to do because of his unwavering commitment to a Vision and his ability to sell that Vision to his employees and investors.

You'll undoubtedly have opportunities to demonstrate your commitment to the organization's Vision and Implementation Plan in the face of adversity. When you do, forgoing the easy way out when it's inconsistent with your Vision and Implementation Plan and insisting on an unwavering pursuit of your Vision will separate your organization from the competition because too many people and organizations settle for less than their full potential. A leader can sometimes force an organization in a direction through sheer will, but your personal commitment to a worthy Vision will accomplish much more. When your people see the organization has heightened expectations because it's committed to a Vision, those people will raise their game to meet those expectations.

I'm guessing Henry Ford's employees took pride in their accomplishments and that the Ford Motor Company developed a sense of *esprit de corps* precisely because it accomplished something that no other car manufacturer had been able to do. We know they had several successes during Henry Ford's tenure. I can't help but believe these successes were due, in part, to the fact that when Ford's employees realized they were part of an innovative organization doing something truly outstanding, they started acting like it.

Take my restaurant example. Once your people buy into the notion that you're going to serve the best steak in town with superior service and an exclusive atmosphere, and that there will be no exceptions or excuses, you'll see them act like they're part of something special. Every customer expects the head waiter at the restaurant serving the best steak in town to be better than the head waiter at an ordinary steakhouse. Your head waiter knows that. They have an image in their mind of the head waiter at the premier steakhouse and the head waiter at an ordinary steakhouse. Whether consciously or not, they'll act like the image they have in their mind of the premier steakhouse's head waiter. (As discussed elsewhere, if they don't, then you should find someone else who will.) When that attitude spreads to the other waiters, positive peer pressure begins to take hold.

I saw that positive peer pressure countless times at Wildcat Oil Tools. Previously I described that in the oilfield, a fisherman is a specially-trained individual who "fishes" a "fish" out of the wellbore. It can be a stressful job. If the fisherman can't recover the fish, and the oil company loses the wellbore, they can easily lose millions of dollars. A fishing job can last several hours and often takes place in difficult physical conditions ranging from cold, dark, and wet nights in the winter, to brutally hot summer days. It takes a special talent and Mindset to handle the stress of the fishermen while finding a solution.

We hired several talented fishermen, and, because of them, we developed a reputation for successfully handling difficult, high-risk fishing jobs. That reputation lead to an institutional confidence. Rather than dread these difficult jobs, our fishermen took the attitude that, "Of course it's a hard job, because if it were easy, they would have called (one of our competitors)." I'm convinced this attitude allowed our guys to recover fish they couldn't have otherwise recovered, because when they arrived at the customer's well site, they knew somehow, someway, they were going to be successful. Thus, when the inevitable setbacks occurred, they weren't deterred. They were convinced they were ultimately going to be successful. Consequently, any setback made for a better story.

CHAPTER 12

As you'll recall, I made sure our fishermen and operators had good trucks, equipment, and uniforms. This choice was not only important to establish the culture of the world's preeminent tool and remedial services company; it also bolstered our fishermen's confidence and self-image. Their confidence and self-image were important for several reasons. When an oil company calls out a fisherman, they frequently have a serious problem and they need a solution right then. Imagine you've become ill and have been sent to a specialist. You're in a treatment room, not feeling well, and are concerned. You're wondering, *what's wrong with me? What will it take to cure this? What if it can't be cured?* At that moment, the most important thing for you is for the doctor to walk into the examination room with a confident smile and attitude that says, "I've got this and you're going to be okay." Our customers wanted to have that same feeling when one of our fishermen arrived on their location. Our team's can-do attitude, coupled with well-maintained equipment and a professional appearance, inspired confidence.

This image and reputation helped us recruit employees, too. Good people want to work for good companies. The type of people that we were interested in would much rather work for the best company in the business than an average company because they were proud of their abilities and they wanted to be part of something in which they could take pride. When they noticed our people and found out a little more about us, they started calling me to ask if I had any openings. As good people left other companies to join us, and they told their friends why, our reputation continued to grow.

So far, I have extolled the virtue of optimism. No worthwhile Vision is possible without it. But your optimism cannot lead you to stick your head in the sand. When problems arise, you should not only have a sense of optimism that the problems can be solved, you must face those problems head-on with a healthy dose of reality, so that you confront the problems and don't ignore them. I've seen this attitude referred to as the Stockdale Paradox.

The Stockdale Paradox is named for the late Vice Admiral James Stockdale. He was a prisoner of war (POW) during the Vietnam War and was the highest-ranking US naval officer to be held as a POW. Because of this high rank, he was put through a special form of hell. For eight years, he lived in solitary confinement in a small cell. The light in his cell stayed on twenty-four hours a day and he was forced to sleep in shackles. Despite these terrible conditions, Admiral Stockdale survived. Many others didn't.

After the war, medical professionals looked for patterns in the survivors and victims. Admiral Stockdale was one of those studied. He explained he combined an objective assessment of his situation with a sense of optimism. He acknowledged to himself that he was in a tough spot, but he knew at some point he would prevail. The prisoners who lacked this balance often didn't survive. For example, some POWs were overly optimistic. They'd tell themselves that they'd be home by Christmas and then when Christmas came and went, they'd tell themselves they'd be home by Easter. When Easter came and went, they'd tell themselves they'd be home by Thanksgiving. After several disappointments, they eventually died of broken hearts.

Admiral Stockdale's willingness to face the reality that he was in hell and that there was nothing that he could do to improve his physical condition or to hasten his release equipped him to deal with his situation. His optimism that he would survive gave him the will not only to persevere but to lift the morale and prolong the lives of his fellow prisoners. For example, he created a tapping code so that the POWs could communicate with one another. He developed a milestone system that helped them deal with torture. In addition, he sent intelligence information hidden in seemingly innocent letters to his wife. Throughout this period of confinement, he kept himself going with an unshakeable belief that somehow, in some way, he would survive and that this experience would be a defining moment in his life.

This approach can also be applied to your organization. There will be times when you face a considerable challenge to your Vision with no obvious solution. If your Vision is lofty, there will definitely be times when your critics publicly doubt your ability to achieve it. When this doubt occurs, you must acknowledge the harsh facts while maintaining an unshakeable belief that you and the organization will ultimately find a solution. The trick is not to let your optimism prevent you from confronting the reality of your situation. In other words, don't simply say to yourself, "I know we're going to survive this," and then stick your head in the sand and hope the problem magically disappears.

There were plenty of times when our Wildcat Oil Tools Vision was challenged. Oil price declines hurt our revenue, our proprietary tools didn't pass factory tests during their design phase, potential transactions that we spent considerable time and money developing fell apart at the eleventh hour, and customers scaled back their drilling plans—right after we had purchased equipment based on their original plan. In each instance, I was confident Wildcat Oil Tools would someday become the world's premier fishing and tool rental company and so I never wavered from my commitment to that Vision. But I didn't let that confidence become a pair of rose-colored glasses that prevented me from seeing the situation as it was.

For example, we encountered significant problems when we started designing our whipstock. We reasonably thought it would be a straightforward task that could be completed within a few months and without incurring significant costs. Our engineers and our design team spent months working on it. Eventually, we built a prototype and started testing it in the lab. The prototype failed. We modified it and retested it. It failed again. Ultimately, we had several modifications before we solved the problem and our whipstock passed its factory tests and field trials. But while we were problem-solving, we had bills to pay with no offsetting income and no guarantee that we would ever have a working design.

In the meantime, we also spent considerable time and money to obtain a patent and trademark, and we put together a marketing campaign. We called our whipstock the XpressDrill. We did some preliminary marketing work during the design phase and then, when we had a working model, we instituted a full-scale marketing campaign. When we started that campaign, we ran into more problems. For example, we put together a social event at a local restaurant to announce our patent application had been granted and that the XpressDrill was officially in service. We reserved the entire restaurant, brought in employees from multiple locations, set up display models, and had videos running on several televisions throughout the restaurant. It was a great idea. Unfortunately, we later learned there was a previously scheduled professional event going on across town at the exact same time as our event. That other event cut into our attendance significantly.

We made numerous sales calls on customers. Many had been supportive while we were designing the XpressDrill. When we started soliciting orders from them, however, they were reluctant to use our whipstock until we had a history of successful runs. It was the old "you can't get a job without experience and you can't get experience without a job" situation.

Even when we had a customer who was willing to consider using the XpressDrill, they inevitably wanted a different size whipstock than the one we were then manufacturing. Wellbores come in various widths. Most run from seven inches to thirteen and three-eighths inches. A whipstock must be designed to fit the size wellbore in which it is being placed. A whipstock designed for a seven-inch wellbore will not work in a nine-inch wellbore. We could have waited until we had developed and manufactured a whipstock for every size wellbore in current use before we started marketing them, but that would have delayed our release considerably, so we opted to start with the most common size whipstocks. For a while, I began to wonder if we would ever have a whipstock size that matched a customer's request.

The entire process was a rollercoaster ride. When a prototype failed a factory test, or I saw updated and increased developmental cost numbers, or a customer said "no," it was discouraging. The process was so discouraging that at times I wondered if we would ever have a successful project. Because we had several other capital demands, I could have justified cancelling the project several times. But that would have effectively killed our entire research and development effort and we couldn't achieve our Vision of becoming a world-class company without a viable research and development department. Giving up, therefore, wasn't an option.

Just as Admiral Stockdale knew he would have to overcome incredible hardship but would eventually be released and allowed to go home, I knew we would have to overcome several challenges, but we would solve the problems as they arose and, therefore, would ultimately have a successful research and development effort. Our research and development and sales departments shared my confidence, which allowed us to set aside our frustrations and to focus on solutions. One by one, we successfully overcame each challenge. We never lost faith in ourselves, but we also never lied to ourselves. When a prototype failed a factory test, or a customer pushed back because our technology was untested, we acknowledged the problem without sugarcoating it.

I'm proud to say today the XpressDrill is a success. We've successfully marketed it in the US and overseas, and the interest in it is increasing, especially internationally. I have no doubt that before long, it will be one of our most successful products. Regardless, the fact that we persevered and saw it through from a concept to a commercial product, is something that I'm proud of, and something that we can draw upon in the future.

The first time you do something challenging, a part of your mind will wonder if you can do it because you've never done it before. That doubt threatens your confidence. But once you do it the first time, that little voice of doubt is gone. Of course, you can do it, after all, you've done it before! The fact that we at Wildcat Oil Tools refused to quit and kept on fighting when we designed the XpressDrill gives us increased confidence to face our future challenges.

CHAPTER THIRTEEN

ETHICS

If we polled one-hundred people and asked them if business leaders should behave ethically, I'm sure every single person would say, "Yes." In fact, I'm sure the group would overwhelmingly respond in favor of any question that suggested behaving ethically was a good thing or should be encouraged. Even if we don't always agree what ethical behavior requires—for example, does it require a commitment to reducing our carbon footprint or actively promoting diversity?—the general principle of encouraging ethical behavior is firmly entrenched in our culture. Every week, churches, synagogues, and mosques across the country extoll the virtue and necessity of high ethical behavior. The stories we read to our children almost always have a moral which encourages ethical behavior. When you watch a movie, the hero is the honest person, the villain is dishonest, and at the end of the movie, the hero is rewarded for their good behavior and the villain suffers because of their bad behavior.

However, if you ask those same one-hundred people if the ethical businessperson always gets the best deal in the negotiations, or other similar questions designed to test whether they believe good ethics makes for a financially successful business, my guess is you'll get a mixture of responses. People want the businesses that they work for and the businesses they deal with to be honest, and they believe being ethical is important for getting into heaven, but I wouldn't be surprised if the group believed dishonest businesspeople frequently get the better of honest businesspeople.

If we asked those who said dishonest businesspeople normally got the better of honest businesspeople, whether they held themselves to an ethical standard, I'm sure everyone would say "yes"—if for no other reason than to avoid embarrassing themselves in front of a pollster. But even if there was a way to guarantee our group was giving an honest response, I'm still confident almost everyone could honestly say, regardless of their subjective belief that dishonest businesspeople have an advantage, they still hold themselves to a higher standard whether because of religious beliefs and their upbringings, among other factors.

If you're one of those individuals who believes dishonest people have an advantage in the business world, I've got good news: you're wrong. Are there times when someone lies or otherwise takes advantage of someone else and appears to get away with it? Of course, but success in business is the sum of many transactions and relationships, and no business prospers over the long term without a solid foundation. Think of Enron. If someone that you're negotiating with lies to you today, how likely are you to do another deal with them in the future? If you are a customer and a business takes advantage of you once, how likely are you to come back? In both situations, how likely are you to tell others about the time you were taken advantage of?

CHAPTER 13

The world is a much smaller place today than it was even a few years ago. Look at your phone. How much information does it give you virtually instantaneous access to? I'll give you an example. I love professional soccer, particularly the top European soccer leagues. If Real Madrid and FC Barcelona are playing in the Champions League, I can watch the game live on my phone and, while the action is slow, I can check the weather in Spain and at home, see what the stock market is doing there and at home, and glance at the news headlines. My phone has my music, pictures, and audiobooks. I use it for directions, to order things, to listen to podcasts, and to send and receive emails and text messages. Sometimes I even use it to make a call. That's a lot of information in the palm of your hand.

This information access has changed our lives. I believe even more significant is our phone's connection to social media platforms. When social media was just getting started, people accessed their Facebook pages at home on their computers. Today, we use our phones to access social media anywhere and at any time. I enjoy social media. I like to post and to see other people's posts. We use social media at Wildcat Oil Tools to promote our business. Because of our international expansion, I now regularly see posts from people all over the world on my phone. Most of the posts that I see are either purely social, or are things to which I pay little attention, but from time to time I see something truly noteworthy. It's not unusual for me to learn about a breaking event through a social media post. My access to social media sites also makes it easier to research someone. Give me basic information about an individual and within minutes I know who they work for, where they went to school, who they are associated with, what they've posted, and what others have said about them.

So, what does our smartphone have to do with ethics? A lot. Do you know what limits dishonest and unethical behavior in the business world? Information. Few will deal with someone they know is dishonest and we're at least reluctant to do business with someone we've been warned about. Our smartphones make it easier for us to communicate with one another. You might get away with deceiving someone once, but you're unlikely to get a second chance to do so. After all, you wouldn't do business again with someone who cheated you once. Nor would you do business with someone if a friend or acquaintance told you that they were dishonest. Because of the number of ways that we have to get and receive information, on our phones alone, it's much easier today to warn others about an unscrupulous person than it's ever been. I can't see that trend reversing itself; in fact, I'd be shocked if the world doesn't continue to shrink.

This world is also smaller because people are more mobile. I don't mean people travel more; rather I mean people normally work for several companies during their careers. That's particularly prevalent in the oil and gas industry because of the business turnover. A business is sold or merged, or it fails, and, as a result, the former employees find new jobs. Let's assume Acme Oil and Gas Company's assets are being sold and an unscrupulous person tries to take unfair advantage of Acme during negotiations. When the sale is closed, Acme will no longer exist, but in a few weeks or months, most of the Acme employees who saw or were otherwise made aware of the unethical behavior are likely to be working at several other companies. If the unscrupulous person tries to negotiate a deal with any of these companies, those former employees are likely to speak up, and the unscrupulous person may find themselves rebuffed and never know why.

As the world shrinks, individual industries do the same. The oil and gas industry is tremendously large and unbelievably small at the same time. There are countless exploration and service companies in the US, let alone the world, and I'm sure I've never heard of most of them. On the other hand, my increased access to information means I have heard of far more industry people and companies, and I can more quickly find out about an unknown company, than I could have a generation ago. People in an industry constantly talk to others in the same industry. Consequently, an unscrupulous person can develop a reputation within the industry more quickly now than at any time in our history. That reputation will open—or close—a lot of doors.

Clearly, there's no doubt that you personally should strive for high ethical behavior for your own benefit. This behavior will also benefit your organization. Your personal ethical behavior, and your insistence that others in the organization behave likewise, will make the organization stronger in numerous ways. First and foremost, you and your senior management team's behavior sets the tone for the organization. Your people are constantly observing your behavior. They naturally assume if it's okay for you to do something, it's okay for them too. Thus, if you come to work late every day, don't be surprised if they straggle in too. On the other hand, if they see you're always at your desk and working well before 8:00 a.m., you can expect the organization will be up and running by eight o'clock every morning.

The same holds true for ethical behavior. If your people see you engage in dishonest behavior or that you tolerate it from a senior manager, don't be surprised if they're not completely honest and forthcoming with you. However, if what they see from you reflects the highest ethical standards and they see you insist on the same from your senior managers, your organization will reflect those standards. People will still make mistakes or have lapses of judgment, and you'll occasionally hire someone who isn't up to your standards, but overall the organization and its reputation will reflect your high standards.

That insistence on high standards will significantly increase your organization's chances for success in numerous ways, for example, by attracting and keeping customers. Let's go back to my steakhouse example. The customer who has a positive experience is far more likely to come back and to encourage their friends to try you out than the customer who has a bad experience. That's particularly true if they feel like they were cheated or taken advantage of. They might forgive you if the waitress made a mistake or it took too long to cook their steak, but they're far less likely to forgive being treated dishonestly.

Ethical businesses have an easier time recruiting and keeping good employees. Let's say you tell your customers that the steaks are 100 percent grass-fed beef, but your employees know that isn't completely true because when your supplier is short of grass-fed beef, you make up the difference with other grades. You can rationalize the situation by saying you try to get 100 percent grass-fed beef and the problem is with the supplier and, besides, after the steak is prepped and cooked, no one can tell the difference. The type of individual that you want to hire and to keep, however, is going to be uncomfortable if they feel any pressure to look the other way.

CHAPTER 13

Good people want to feel good about themselves. Who we work for and what we do is a big part of how we feel about ourselves. Think of what it must have felt like to have been a part of NASA during the moon landings versus being a part of Enron after news of its problems broke. If a company doesn't do business ethically, a good person is going to find somewhere else to work, and they're going to tell their friends why they left. On the other hand, if someone is proud to work for a company because of what that company represents, they're going to share that pride, too. Give me a team of honest, hardworking individuals, and I'll take on any other business anywhere and at any time.

Ethically-run companies have a much easier time attracting top-quality investors and joint venturers. Ask yourself, how likely would you be to invest in a company that you knew was being dishonest with its employees, customers, or lenders? If you've made it this far in my book, the answer is that it wouldn't happen. You wouldn't invest your money because you wouldn't want to be associated with the unethical business and because you want your investment to succeed. You'd be justifiably concerned this business could ultimately suffer the same fate as Enron's. For that same reason, if you had a chance to enter into a joint venture with another business, and you knew or suspected it had ethical issues, you'd look elsewhere. Other investors and businesspeople would make the same decision. And as the world continues to shrink, potential investors and joint venturers will have greater access to information about how your business operates. That's one of the many reasons why your reputation and your organization's reputation are so important and must be protected.

My general counsel likes to point out that ethically-run businesses have less financial exposure for litigation costs, judgments, and fines. Unfortunately, there is no way to conduct business and guarantee you'll never be sued. We carry insurance to protect ourselves, our employees, our customers, and those with whom we interact. Beyond that, if we treat people fairly, our chances of being sued and having a judgment rendered against us are far less than the chances of a businessperson who lacks morals or who tries to push everything to the edge. When you try to take advantage of people, they often find a way to strike back.

You've probably heard people say oral contracts are unenforceable and, therefore, merely because they made an oral promise to do something doesn't mean they're legally obligated to keep their promise. I realize the people who do this normally phrase it differently to make themselves look better, but for those on the other side, there's no doubt about this individual's intention. My general counsel tells me that there are, in fact, times when an oral contract is enforceable. Regardless, if you make an oral promise and honor it, you've got no reason to worry about going to court. On the other hand, the person who pushes the envelope by doing things such as disavowing oral promises on the grounds that they weren't reduced to writing, will often find themselves in court. I'm no lawyer, but my guess is that when this happens, the judge will be looking for a way to make them responsible. Letting someone make and break a promise simply because it was oral offends our notion, including a judge's notion, of right and wrong.

Ethical business practices lower compliance costs. Every business operates under some regulation. There is nothing wrong with min-

CHAPTER 13

imizing the cost of compliance. For example, at Wildcat Oil Tools we pay the taxes and fees that we owe and not one cent more. There are times when we could get away with doing even less. Because the government can't enforce every rule in every instance, it's possible to ignore a regulation or submit a false document and get away with it. That falsification can be tempting when a regulation is nonsensical, or it imposes a burden out of proportion to any benefit. But, like people who push the envelope in their contractual situations generally spend more time in court than others, people who try to get away with ignoring rules and regulations run some serious risks that someday they'll get caught. If so, whatever savings they received will be quickly eaten up by legal bills, interest, penalties, and fines.

Throughout this chapter I've equated ethics with honesty. I appreciate that being ethical requires more than simply being honest. I started with honesty because in my experience, most ethical dilemmas in business involve a challenge to act honestly or the consequences of not acting honestly. Ethical business practices are honest practices. Good business ethics also require treating employees well, helping those who cannot help themselves, and being a good corporate citizen.

I'll use my steakhouse to give you some quick examples of the things that ethical businesses do to illustrate my point. Assume the minimum working age in the community is sixteen years old. You'd never dream of hiring a thirteen-year-old to wash dishes. (Let's exclude family members helping the family-owned restaurant from this discussion. I'm talking about a non-family member dropping out of school and going to work as a full-time employee.) One day a uniform salesman shows up. You talk to him and realize he can provide you with all of your uniform needs at a fraction of the cost you're currently paying. He's brought a sample and you check it out. Everything appears to be of high quality and you're now definitely interested. Then you notice the label says, "Manufactured in Bangladesh." You've recently seen a news story describing the high incidence of child labor in Bangladesh. That article said many of these child laborers are being forced to work in garment factories. What do you do?

You could stick your head in the sand. You don't know that the factory that makes these uniforms uses child laborers. There are probably lots of garment factories in Bangladesh that don't use children, and this salesman and his company appear legitimate. You tell yourself that surely, this company wouldn't take advantage of kids. On the other hand, you could rationalize the situation. Even if this factory uses child laborers, they're paying those kids for their work and their families need the money. If the factory is forced out of business, you'll hurt the children and their families more.

If you stick your head in the sand or lie to yourself, what do you see when you look in the mirror? Is that who you are? So, keeping in mind that this is the real world, what do you do? One option is to tell the salesman why you're bothered and ask him for written verification that his company complies with international law by not using child laborers. If his company is legitimate, he shouldn't have any trouble giving you something in writing confirming their commitment to avoid using child laborers. I promise you that if their uniforms are manufactured in Bangladesh, you aren't the first person to ask him about child laborers and if they're conducting their business ethically, they're happy to confirm that in writing. If

CHAPTER 13

he does anything else, such as deflect the question or simply offer his verbal assurance, then you thank him for his time and show him the door.

Here's another example. Ethical businesses treat their employees and vendors with respect. That treatment requires more than following the law. Ethical businesses don't discriminate against someone because of age, race, or religion; they pay people what they owe them; and they provide safe working environments. Ethical businesses also strive to eliminate harassment. There are times at Wildcat Oil Tools when we have to be stern with people because in our business mistakes can get people killed, and I don't mind hurting someone's feelings if it'll save a life later, but there's a difference between reading someone the riot act after they've made a mistake that put others at risk, and harassing someone simply because you can.

A business shows respect to its employees and vendors by listening to them and by addressing their concerns. Not only is behaving respectfully the right thing to do, when you listen to your employees and vendors, you'll learn about problems and opportunities that you might not have known about otherwise. When you address their concerns, you earn loyalty that you'll almost certainly need in the future. I've had a couple of vendors go above and beyond to bail me out of a situation because I had helped them in the past.

Let's end this chapter with the good news. The things that your parents taught you to do, the things that you do because they feel right, and the things that you've taught your children to do, are good business practices. Be honest, insist your people act honestly, and treat others with respect. You'll not only never regret it, but someday you'll look back and be grateful that you did.

CHAPTER FOURTEEN

NEVER STAND STILL

In both business and in life, there's no such thing as maintaining the status quo. You're either improving or you're falling behind the competition. That adage is definitely true in America. The American free market system isn't perfect, but it's far better than anything that I've seen in my international travels at promoting efficiency and providing opportunity. How many countries would give a kid who arrived without being able to speak the local language, and who worked in onion fields and mowed yards, an opportunity to study at a major university? What country would then give that same person an opportunity to start a business from scratch and grow it into an international company? The answer is, not many countries.

If you've never engaged in business in another country, it's difficult to appreciate how easy our system makes it to start and operate a business. My general counsel tells me that in an emergency, he can incorporate a business, get a tax identification number, and open a bank account—all in one day. If I give him a week, he simply laughs and asks when I'll have something hard for him to do. It's easy to take this for granted but the reality is that in many other parts of the world an individual cannot start a new business without first going through a time-consuming, expensive, bureaucratic maze. That's one of the reasons why you don't see as many start-ups with innovative ideas outside the US.

There's another side to the coin, however. In the US, businesses are allowed to fail, and every year thousands of US businesses do fail. I know right now some of you are saying, "Okay, maybe that's true for smaller businesses, but what about all the government bailouts?" I've got some strong opinions about the bailouts to which you're probably referring. My opinions are no doubt fueled by the fact that, to my knowledge, no American conventional energy company has ever received a penny of government bailout money. Instead, the bailouts always seem to go to Wall Street, but those bailouts represent a tiny fraction of the American businesses that have found themselves in trouble. For the overwhelming, vast majority of the American businesses who find themselves unable to pay their debts, there is no bailout. We have bankruptcy laws that give individual debtors some protection from their creditors and that offer businesses the opportunity to reorganize or to liquidate in an orderly manner. Otherwise, no matter how hard you work or how good your products and services are, if your business cannot pay its bills, it will ultimately be forced to close.

Even though I'm aggravated at the preferential treatment some businesses get from Congress, I don't want to see Congress start bailing out more companies. Quite the opposite. I want all businesses to be treated equally no matter where their headquarters are or what products and services they provide. The truth is, I'd rather that there be no bailouts than to see Congress start bailing out American energy companies, because I think being allowed to fail is one of the reasons why American businesses are so well run.

Let's go back to my steakhouse example. Every year there will probably be several restaurants in your town that fail and close their doors. Don't want to be one of those? Then run your restaurant well. That means serving good food, providing superior service, and offering competitive prices—all while constantly watching your costs. The restaurants that can't pull off every one of these tasks lose business to those who can. Over time, the poorest performers will close. Who benefits the most from this cycle? American restaurant customers. This culling process, while harsh for restaurant owners, maximizes an American consumer's access to efficient, well-run restaurants.

Allowing companies to fail provides several other benefits as well. For example, it focuses our country's talent where it can best be utilized. Imagine a software design company goes under because it didn't control its costs, or it didn't develop popular software products. Odds are that it had some talented employees. They now need jobs and would usually apply with other software design companies. The companies who are most likely to be hiring are either successful companies that are expanding or new companies with innovative ideas. Both groups need additional employees and, in my experience, would prefer to find individuals with prior experience. Consequently, you'll frequently see people who lost their jobs when their employer failed wind up working for other companies in the same industry. American consumers benefit when they do.

The established, growing company is presumably producing something that American consumers want and is selling it at a competitive price. The start-up company normally has an innovative idea that it is starting to market. Because both groups are expanding, they need additional talent. Many of the people who were laid off have the talent and experience these groups need. When these individuals apply for new jobs, their talent will be put to work. If they go to work for an established company, this talent will help it continue to expand. If they go to work for a start-up, their talent increases the chances their new employer will successfully market its innovative idea.

If the former employees can't find a job with other software companies, they will inevitably apply with successful companies in other areas, since those companies are hiring. That, too, is good for our economy because it directs talent to opportunity. When the Ford Motor Company took off, there were still companies making horse-drawn carriages. If you worked for one, seeing your employer fail as people started buying motor cars instead of horse-drawn carriages had to cause you anxiety. While I feel for people in that situation, obviously the country as a whole benefitted when our talented people started designing, manufacturing, and servicing automobiles instead of horse-drawn carriages.

Finally, allowing companies to fail allocates our capital better. If you're purchasing stock as an investment, you're looking for a stock that will appreciate. If you're a commercial loan officer at a bank you're looking for a borrower that will repay your loan in a timely manner with interest. Ultimately, both the investor and loan officer are looking for the same thing: a well-run company that will take their capital and use it to generate a profit. When the banker and investor believe they've found such a company, they infuse it with capital. If the company performs poorly, the investor sells its stock

CHAPTER 14

and invests the proceeds elsewhere. If the company fails to repay the loan, the bank forecloses on the collateral and lends the proceeds to another company. In either instance, capital is steered from unsuccessful ventures to successful ones. That may mean capital flows from a poorly-run company to a well-run one in the same industry or from a struggling industry to a growing one. Regardless, our capital will be invested in the companies and industries with the best opportunity to succeed.

My description of talent and capital being redirected may sound painless. That's not correct. At times the American system can seem brutal and unfair. For example, when oil prices fall, American energy companies often respond by cutting back on the number of employees. If you're one of those who is laid off, the anxiety is compelling because even though you did nothing wrong, you're now out of a job, you have a family to provide for, and the prospects for another job are limited. You might have to take a cut in pay, change careers, look for a job outside the oil and gas industry, or even move to another city. As I've noted, this process ultimately steers talent and capital to opportunity. That process is good for the American economy but for the people who are the victims of this reallocation, I'm sure that knowledge is of limited comfort. I can also understand why some would conclude we should alter the system to soften the blow for these individuals. However, I've personally seen other countries try to do this and, in the process, they've done more harm than good.

For example, I've seen the instance where the government owned the banks and it evaluated them based on the number of jobs they helped create, rather than on whether their loans were being repaid.

On first blush, encouraging job creation would appear to be a good idea. As you can imagine, however, when group one showed up at the bank wanting to borrow money to build a factory that would employ two hundred people but didn't have a good business plan and group two wanted to borrow money to start a business that would employ twenty people but did have a good business plan, that business plan was almost immaterial because the bank would rather tell its regulators that it created two hundred jobs rather than twenty jobs. You can also guess what ultimately happened. The factory owners got a loan and used it to build a factory that eventually failed. Their two hundred employees now needed new jobs. The group with the good business plan didn't get a loan and, therefore, didn't start their business. At the end of the day, people were unemployed, capital was wasted, and an opportunity was lost.

I've also seen countries where labor groups were extremely powerful try to cushion the impact of job losses by first, making it difficult to let someone go and then, by requiring employers to provide a considerable severance package when an employee was terminated. Right now you might be asking, what's wrong with limiting arbitrary employer decisions and providing people who were laid off with financial assistance while they look for work? Believe it or not, this effort to be compassionate results in higher unemployment.

Before I explain my reasoning, let me make one thing clear. The American business system makes it legally easy to let someone go but 99 percent of the people that I've been associated with find reductions in force horribly difficult to do and only implement a layoff when there's no other option. I'm sure that's of limited comfort to the people who have been laid off, but in my experience American employers feel a sense of moral responsibility for their employees and they act accordingly.

Let's get back to why the government-imposed compassion measures hurt employment. Consider our steakhouse. Business is growing and you're considering adding staff. However, the growth hasn't been steady, you've had a mix of high-volume days followed by slow days, and there is a new restaurant scheduled to open nearby. Consequently, you're concerned if you add staff now, you'll end up overstaffed and will have to cut back on hours or lay people off. If you're in the country that makes it difficult and expensive to let people go, the decision is easy. You don't hire anyone unless you're absolutely certain you need them and unless you're positive they meet your need.

In America, the fact that you can reduce your workforce if necessary helps employment in two ways. First, you're more likely to expand your workforce when there's less risk to do so, and vice versa. Second, you're more likely to take a chance on an individual when you have an acceptable option if they fail. Imagine you've decided to expand the kitchen staff by giving your chef an executive assistant. You've got an individual with potential but no experience. If you know you can let them go without first getting the government's permission or without being required to provide a large severance package if they fail to perform, you're much more likely to give them an opportunity. If this sounds cold-hearted, ask yourself: when you were just starting out, did anyone ever give you an opportunity to prove yourself? Where would you be today if they hadn't? Thus, shouldn't we encourage businesses to give people a chance to prove themselves?

I started this chapter by saying you should never stand still. Obviously one reason to stay moving is to avoid failure. Even if you never fail, however, settling for the status quo means you've adopted a ceiling for your organization and your people. I don't care what type of organization that you're responsible for, there's something that you need from others, and these people have options. If you stand still long enough, they'll eventually decide one of your competitors—who isn't standing still—is a better option.

If you run a business, this concept is easy to see and understand. If you are the unquestioned leader in your field today, but you fail to evolve, your competition will eventually catch and then pass you. When your customers have the option of getting a better product or service at a more competitive price, they'll do so. This concept also applies to non-profits. Let's say you are the leader of a non-profit organization. You need donations and volunteers to run your organization. Donors and volunteers want to support worthwhile causes, and they want to feel their contributions are making a difference. If your organization becomes stagnant, you run the risk that another organization will see an unmet need, will step in to address that need, and that your donors and volunteers will be more excited by it than your organization and will shift their donations and time to it.

Another reason to avoid stagnation is that otherwise your employees' growth suffers. Wildcat's growth meant our employees had to grow as well. When we expanded our product lines, many of our frontline employees and all of our managers had to learn about the new products. Those who were directly involved in the new products had to become experts on them. All of our yards grew,

CHAPTER 14

so if you were managing a yard, your personnel responsibilities increased. If you were responsible for a product line or division, your geographic responsibilities increased as we added facilities.

We tried to push that growth even further with our quality management system, or QMS. I mentioned earlier that our written job processes were the key component of our Implementation Plan and that as we grew, those processes became part of our quality management system. We spent a considerable amount of time, effort, and money developing a QMS that not only minimized the risk of us sending a defective or incorrect product to the field but also caused us to focus continually on improving our products and services. We developed and then improved processes, procedures, and standards. We conducted internal audits to verify QMS compliance and we held quarterly manager meetings to review the audits and to discuss improvements. Throughout this process, we emphasized what was good enough last year wasn't good enough for this year and definitely wouldn't be good enough next year. Our analysis always started with the assumption that there had to be a better way to identify and meet our customers' expectations. When a meeting starts with a question, and the assumption that there is an answer to that question, it's funny how often someone comes up with a good answer. On the other hand, if you allow what you're doing now is good enough to be an acceptable answer, don't be surprised how often the answer "good enough" is chosen.

The continued drive for improvement not only improved Wildcat Oil Tools, it also improved our people. They knew we fully expected them to find ways to improve and so they spent considerable time looking at their area of operations for possible improvements. They looked outside for possible innovations. They talked to one another and swapped ideas. This type of thinking not only prevented them from becoming stagnant in their jobs, it made them better at their areas of responsibility.

Some people thrive in an environment that stresses growth. Others don't thrive because they get comfortable or they're afraid of change. Our Vision was completely inconsistent with a fear of change or a resistance to growth. Therefore, I didn't allow someone who was unwilling to get outside their comfort zone to remain in a position where they could hold us back.

Avoiding stagnation is also important for you, personally. To make sure I'm not becoming stagnant, I am always looking for a new goal. For example, every year I set a goal to lower my golf handicap by a set number of strokes by the end of the summer. If you're a runner, you might focus on running farther or faster this year than last. If you have a hobby, your goal could be related to that hobby. I don't think the subject of your goal matters one iota. The key is to have a goal that excites you and that requires effort on your part to achieve.

One of my recent goals was to learn Italian. That's not the easiest thing to do in west Texas or in the oil business generally, because you rarely encounter someone speaking Italian. However, the goal was important to me and so I found time each day to work on and practice my Italian. Eventually, I even changed my iPhone's language from English to Italian. That certainly improved my Italian, but it also caused some consternation at work. When I forwarded an email or a text to someone else at Wildcat Oil Tools, I had to make sure that it came through in English. Occasionally I'd forget, and I'd get a call asking, "What in the world is this?" Once my general counsel,

CHAPTER 14

Rick Strange, and I attended an oil and gas conference. The conference included a golf tournament one morning. When we left the hotel for the golf course, he drove, and I navigated. I set my iPhone to give us directions. Those directions were of course in Italian. Rick gave me a "What the—?" look and so I explained what I was doing. Rick doesn't speak Italian, so I'd have to translate, and, in the process, we missed a couple of turns. When the tournament was over, and we got in the car to head to the hotel, I grabbed my phone, but Rick insisted on using his English-speaking phone. (We didn't miss any turns on the way back, but Rick missed out on expanding his horizons.)

Will my knowledge of Italian ever pay off in the business world? Who knows? Stranger things have obviously happened. But even if I never use my Italian for business, I'm convinced I'm a better person for the experience. The time that I spent working on Italian was time that I wasn't spending vegetating in front of a television. No one doubts the benefit of exercise for our physical health. The same holds true for our mind. Learning a new language was an invaluable mental exercise for me. Moreover, it was a positive example. When I slipped and sent something in Italian to someone else at work, I'd eventually have to explain what I was doing. Word soon spread to our managers. None of them attempted to learn Italian, but I like to think that my goal led them to find a goal that motivated them to improve their minds.

I also set work goals for myself. For example, at the beginning of the year I'll set a goal to increase our business from a particular account, to find a way to lower our costs of goods sold for a particular product, or to add a product line. These personal goals help me stay motivated and focused. I encourage you to do the same.

Another good example of using goals to achieve your Vision is to set team goals for different groups within your organization. To be successful, first ask yourself, what behavior do I want to incentivize? The oilfield can be dangerous and unfortunately people are sometimes tempted to take shortcuts that increase the danger. To combat unsafe practices, many oil and gas companies utilize incentive-based programs to promote safety. For example, a company might announce that their goal is to go X days without an on-the-job injury. If an office or division achieves this goal, then everyone in that office or division receives a reward. If the organization as a whole achieves the goal, then everyone receives an award. When properly done, these programs can promote a safer workplace.

After you've decided what behavior you're going to incentivize, make the target specific and measurable. "Having a safer workplace," "improving customer satisfaction," and "becoming healthier" are all worthwhile, but they're too broad to serve as real goals. Instead, you could consider, "Having zero on-the-job injuries requiring medical treatment this year," "Achieving three stars in a published rating guide," or "Reducing the number of sick days taken this year by X days."

Then ask yourself, is there a risk of unintended consequence? For example, if your goal is to reduce the number of sick days taken this year, are you going to have sick employees show up to work when they should be staying home getting well? They will if the prize is significant enough. So, in this instance, maybe you achieve your goal of having a healthier workforce if you announce there will be a five-kilometer fun run-and-walk in six months and that if X number of employees successfully complete the event, there will be a reward for the entire company.

CHAPTER 14

Team goals should promote team activity. If I set a goal to sell X number of whipstocks during a quarter, I've incentivized my whipstock salesmen but probably no one else. If it's my salesmen that I'm worried about, then that's fine. However, if I can find a goal that incentives a broader group and, better yet, if I can find a way to foster some healthy competition between facilities or divisions, I will improve Wildcat's performance. I believe the better your people work together, the better their collective work product will be.

Make the process of achieving a goal fun. Everyone will know you have an ulterior motive when you announce the goal. That knowledge can lead to a certain amount of cynicism. Thus, if you're trying to change behavior, you need people to buy in. Some companies try to purchase buy-in. They'll announce a program and will offer a phenomenal prize. Obviously, that works—at least during the program—which is one of the reasons why companies use it. However, I'd rather change long-term behavior and I believe you're much more likely to achieve this with a fun program.

For example, assume we've hit a stretch where the average time between the date a service is provided, and when we get paid gets too long. (For simplicity I'll simply refer to this as "lag.") I could get on my soapbox and start jumping on my managers, or I could go to individual facilities and walk through their processes to see where we could improve our performance, or I could use a carrot. Obviously, there is a time to hold managers accountable for performance, and the CEO should always understand what's going on in the field and why, but in this instance, there may be a better way to solve the lag problem using a goal-and-reward system.

Let's use the steps that I outlined above to see if such a system is possible. What's the behavior that I want to incentivize? Broadly speaking, I want to improve cashflow by getting paid faster and so anything that encourages people to get bills out faster, or to improve the accuracy of our bills, or encourages people to communicate with customers about our billing, is important. Is such a goal measurable? Generally, yes. Our accounting department records reflect the date services were provided and when an invoice was paid. I can determine the difference in time between each invoice and its payment and I can calculate an average for all our invoices. Is this average sufficiently specific? Probably not for individual employees, because it's not immediately apparent what individual behavior I'm targeting or what they need to do to earn the reward. I could get into the weeds and develop specific goals for individual groups. If I spent enough time and energy on it, I could probably develop a program that would work. But what if I made the effort into a team competition and let my employees find solutions?

I can calculate the lag, not only for the company as a whole, but for each individual facility as well. If I announced a contest with the prize going to the facility that achieved the biggest reduction in its lag, I'm more apt to achieve buy-in because I've empowered my managers and employees. They know the general problem and they know what they do that impacts lag. Until now, it has been easy for them to consider this lag the company's problem. However, there's now a prize if they can help find and implement a solution. We'll talk about the prize more later, but let's assume it's something they want. If so, their facility's lag has started to become their problem and it's up to them to figure out how to reduce the lag. If a particular facility identifies a solution, it becomes their solution. That's important because they're much more likely to follow their solution consistently than a solution that I've forced upon them, and they're more likely to hold each other accountable if the team has to succeed to earn the prize.

Is such a contest fun? Some people are naturally more competitive than others, but almost everyone enjoys being part of a group striving for a group goal. There are several ways to provide the group with a tangible reward that encourages a team commitment. One way that I avoid is putting the members of the winning group in a drawing and then picking one person. Then, although the whole group earned the distinction, only one individual truly benefits. You can offer a nice prize when you do this, but I'd rather see the team enjoy the award together.

In our situation, because the teams consist of individual facilities, we could have a cookout at the winning facility, or give everyone at that facility some extra paid time off. Either reward would work and both would be appreciated. However, when I'm promoting a team activity, I personally like to give the winners something more permanent that distinguishes them from the rest of the company. The military has this method down to an artform. If you're a Navy SEAL, you get to wear a Trident on your uniform. If you're an Army Ranger, you wear a Ranger Tab. If you're a pilot, you wear a set of wings. Each of these items only costs the military a few cents to purchase, but it's unbelievable the commitment that people make to earn the right to wear one of them.

You can achieve a similar result in your organization without spending significant money. For example, I could give the winners of the reduce-the-lag contest each a nice coat, suitable for wearing to work. This group would be the only people in the organization to ever receive this particular coat. The coat becomes a sense of team pride because it serves as a reminder of the group's accomplishment. Also, that coat can also serve as an incentive for the rest of the company because of envy—not as much envy of the coat itself, as envy of the recognition.

If your organization is small, an intramural competition might be impossible or even counterproductive. In that case, find a goal that pits your organization against the competition or compares this year's performance against last year's. Regardless of your approach, if you're creative, you can find something that encourages collaborative behavior and which will force your organization to stretch itself to achieve.

CHAPTER FIFTEEN

PERSONAL HABITS

Good leaders are disciplined in their personal lives. If not, their organization suffers. I've previously discussed how critical your commitment to the organization's Vision and Implementation Plan is. If you're not completely committed to that Vision and Plan, you'd probably be better served to forget it. On the other hand, your commitment will provide a measure of organizational discipline because it encourages decisions and actions consistent with the Vision and Plan and it discourages those which are not. That Vision discipline is important, but when I say personal life discipline, I mean something else.

Make healthy decisions. You've heard countless times that it's important to work out and to eat healthy food. You know that those who do so are much more likely to live long and happy lives than those who do not. I can't give you any statistics, but my impression is most people do not work out regularly, and that too many of us eat too many hamburgers and too few fruits and vegetables. Trust me, I'm no angel on either account, but I do take pride in my exercise and eating habits and I'm convinced your leadership skills will improve with good health and will suffer with bad health.

There are the obvious reasons why a healthy lifestyle will make you a better leader. First, healthy people spend more productive time at work than unhealthy people. It's difficult to be an effective leader if you're home—or worse, hospitalized—because of an illness. Everyone catches a cold now and then, but too many Americans suffer from preventable diseases such as obesity, type-two diabetes, hypertension, and cardiovascular disease. For many, poor lifestyle choices played a role either in the onset or the severity of these illnesses. Conversely, if you work out, eat the right foods, and get enough sleep, you're far less likely to suffer any of these. If you stay healthy, you'll have more time to do the things that you enjoy and spend a lot less time seeking medical treatment. In addition, the time you spend at work will be more productive.

Secondly, you're an example. Want your people to lead healthy lifestyles? Don't let them see you eating donuts every morning at your desk. Instead, let them see you doing the things you'd like them to do. Obviously, people must make their own lifestyle choices; but peer pressure—good and bad—affects those choices. When you do the right thing and you encourage others to do the same, your example and prodding have an effect. Maybe you'll change one person's habits at first, but it's a start and success breeds success. You may be surprised to see that healthy choices can become a part of the organization's culture.

Third, healthy people are more productive. I like to work out before work. I don't always make it, but I've noticed when I do, I feel better physically, and I feel better about myself emotionally. I also have more energy and a sharper mind. The same holds true for when I'm eating well. I have an occasional cheat meal, and even though a nutritionist might disagree, I don't think a hamburger every now and then is a problem. However, when I'm on a streak of eating well versus letting the occasional cheat meal become a pattern, I definitely notice the change in my energy. Higher energy levels allow me to focus better, avoid distractions, and remain alert all day.

Fourth, healthy people, including those who have recently improved their lifestyle and are seeing positive changes, are happier than less healthy people. It's hard to be happy when you're ill and incapable of doing the things you enjoy. Beyond happiness, people feel better about themselves when they exercise positive control over their circumstances. For example, it's tempting to eat dessert and as long as it's an occasional treat, there's no problem. However, when that dessert becomes more than an occasional treat, the inevitable post-slip guilt lowers your self-esteem. You start to tell yourself that your lack of discipline is a sign that you're a bad person. If you let that guilt build, soon your self-image suffers. It's hard to be happy when you keep telling yourself that you're a weak person.

Earlier I described why Admiral McRaven, a highly decorated Navy SEAL, promotes the benefits of something simple like correctly making your bed when you get up. Making one's bed is a little thing, but nonetheless it's an accomplishment and beginning the day with a sense of accomplishment promotes a positive self-image. For me, starting the day with a workout not only helps physically, but mentally, too, because the feeling of accomplishment carries over and gives me a sense of optimism. It's easier for me to take on the day's challenges when that little voice in my head is celebrating a good workout instead of berating me for sleeping in.

Working out consistently isn't easy. If it were, everyone would work out regularly. To make it easier, find something that you enjoy, participate in a group when you can, and set a goal. I play racquetball some mornings with a group of guys that get together every day at 6:00 a.m. and play for an hour. As they like to point out, you can spend an hour playing racquetball and be surprised when someone says it's seven o'clock because you've been having so much fun. If you get on a cardio machine, on the other hand, you'll be looking at your watch every five minutes wondering why the time is passing so slowly. If racquetball isn't your thing, find something else that is. It's a lot easier to stay motivated to continue doing something that you enjoy than it is doing something you dread.

Participating in a group helps because you've got someone to help hold you accountable. If I promise the racquetball group that I'll play on Monday, but I fail to show up, I know I'll hear about it Tuesday, Wednesday, Thursday, and so on. Knowing I'm accountable makes it a lot easier for me to get up when the alarm goes off Monday morning and I'm tempted to hit the snooze button. Groups also provide support and encouragement when you need it, and for many, it's more fun to work out with a group than it is to go to the gym and get on a cardio machine by yourself.

It's important to be realistic when you plan your workout regimen. I work out in the morning because I can and also that's the best time of day for me. If you're a committed night owl, though, or you're responsible for getting the kids to school, my routine may not work for you. If you start your fitness program by trying to work out at an unrealistic time, at a minimum you're making your new habit unnecessarily difficult. In all likelihood, that difficulty will eventually derail your workout plan. A more realistic option for you may be to walk during your lunch hour, or to stop at the gym on the way home from work. Whatever that convenient time is for you, use it.

Set goals. I'm a big believer in goals because they work. I've used them at Wildcat Oil Tools to encourage our folks to stretch themselves and improve their performance. A good work goal automatically changes personal behavior. The same holds true for workouts. I love to play golf and I want to see myself improve every year. I can tell myself in January that this year I'm going to play better. If so, I might or might not improve. On the other hand, I can set a goal—for example, to lower my handicap two strokes. If I set a realistic goal and hold myself accountable for it, I'll automatically change my behavior. Instead of mindlessly hitting golf balls at the range, I'll focus on a specific part of my game and will more closely monitor my performance. Instead of monitoring how far I hit my driver, I'll pay attention to what part of my game most needs improvement. That act of attention results in my spending time practicing putting and chipping or working on some other specific area of my game. What's more, the whole time I'll be having fun because I'm focused on my goal.

Consequently, don't say, "This year I'm going to get into shape." Set a goal. Maybe it's a commitment to run your first marathon; or if you're just beginning, you can commit to completing a five-kilometer run. Whatever the goal, make sure it's challenging but realistic, that it's measurable, and then tell people about it. I'm much more likely to show up for racquetball knowing my buddies will give me grief if

I don't. You want your friends and loved ones to encourage you when you need it, to give you a little grief when you start to slack off, and to help you celebrate when you successfully complete your goal.

Get enough rest. It's also important to get adequate rest. I've heard numerous recommendations for the number of hours of sleep that your body needs to perform at its best. I suspect the correct answer varies for different people. For me, it's eight hours a night. One thing that I do know about sleep is that getting enough doesn't just happen. It's the classic dilemma of, "If you fail to plan, you plan to fail." That means setting, and sticking to, a regular bedtime routine and adopting habits that will allow you to fall asleep quickly and get a good night's rest.

For me, those habits include no caffeine at night, and avoiding television and the phone for two hours before bedtime. This habit can be difficult to keep. We get home from work, we're tired, and we sit down and turn on the television. Then that television frequently stays on, even if there's nothing that we want to watch, until we go to bed. We've become accustomed to using our phones incessantly to check emails, send and receive text messages, check the weather and the day's sports scores, participate in social media sites, and on and on. (Occasionally, some of us still use them to talk.) I've read that exposure to television and phone screens interferes with our sleep patterns. Apparently, our bodies are still programmed to go to sleep when the sun sets and to get up when it rises. Exposure to television and phone screens can lead our body to thinking that the sun is still up. I've personally noticed when I turn off the television and set aside my phone a couple of hours before bed, I go to sleep faster and easier.

CHAPTER 15

Fortunately, technology has made turning the television off and setting the phone aside easier. If your plan is to turn the television off at eight o'clock, but there's something coming on at nine that you'd like to see, you can record it and watch it tomorrow without having to sit through the commercials. Most of us now have televisions and DVRs that make recording a show or series so easy that you no longer need a teenager to explain how to use them. Your phone is even easier. Every email, text message, and social media post that is sent to you after you set down the phone will still be there tomorrow morning without you having to do anything.

Make your calendar match your priorities. I'm continually bombarded with emails, text messages, phone calls, and social media posts. If I'm not careful, I can look up at the end of the day and realize I lost control of my time because I spent all of it responding to others. The only way to avoid that is with some personal discipline. In this case, that means prioritizing your time.

Unfortunately, you can't pre-plan all of your time. Emergencies and unexpected developments will happen; and if you don't return your customer's phone calls or emails, they'll eventually find someone else who will. However, you can decide what must happen on a particular day, week, or month and then plan accordingly. Maybe you'll create a to-do list and make it a habit to complete everything on that list in an appointed time. I like to-do lists because they automatically cause you to prioritize your time. For example, you've got three things on your day's to-do list. You knock off the first two before lunch. After lunch, a distraction arises. It's not an emergency; it's truly a distraction. If you've done nothing to structure your day, the distraction will take control of your time. If you're committed to finishing the last item on your to-do list, though, you'll find yourself ignoring the distraction until you finish that last item.

If you decide to use a to-do list in this manner, keep in mind a few pointers. First, your list must represent the items that are essential to do in the appointed time. If the list becomes too long because you've combined items that have to be done with things that you'd like to get done, the list losses its authority and you'll stop using it to prioritize your time. Second, pick a reasonable but short period of time for working off the items. If you give yourself too much time, it becomes easy to procrastinate because unconsciously you know you can.

Calendars allow me to plan ahead. For example, if I need to cover something with managers, scheduling a time for a meeting or conference call and blocking that time on my calendar means not only that I'll protect that time, but I'll necessarily plan my other commitments around it. Calendars are also useful for me because I travel a lot. Some of my trips are more important than others, and some of my travel arrangements are more flexible than others. I make sure to block off time at least for the important and nonflexible travel. Flexible travel and commitments will then automatically be planned around the trips I have to take.

Establish a time to deal with the details. Even the most disciplined person that I know, has something that they procrastinate instead of doing. For most of us, it's dealing with details. Maybe it's completing or reviewing a report, reading a proposed contract, or responding to emails. Whatever it may be, each of us has something that we need to do, don't enjoy doing, and find it easy to postpone. A quick solution is to pick a time that you'll use for taking care of the daily details. Maybe it's first thing in the morning before the emails and phone calls take over. For others, it may be during the noon hour. Whatever that time is, designate it as your details time.

For most, I'd recommend you avoid picking the end of the day to take care of your details. Even if everything in your schedule has gone well that day, by the end of the day you're tired and you're naturally thinking of what you'll do when you leave the office. Thus, not only will you not be able to give the details your best effort, there will too frequently be opportunities to delay them until tomorrow. If your day's schedule hasn't gone well, you may never get to your details time because your day spilled over into that time.

Do your least favorite first. Imagine you've set aside time for the details, or you've been out of the office and when you return you've got phone calls to return or emails to which to respond. In either event, assume you've got five things to accomplish today. Odds are good that one or two of these are things that you know you'll enjoy, such as a phone call to a happy customer. In addition, odds are that there is at least one task that you're dreading, such as a phone call to an unhappy customer. If so, take care of that one first.

This strategy works for several reasons. If it's something that you're dreading, you're going to be thinking about it anyway and so the longer you procrastinate, the longer it'll be a distraction and an energy-drainer. Frequently, for me, the anticipation proves worse than the actual event. Thus, the sooner that I mark this off my to-do list, the quicker I'll be able to focus all my attention on other items, and vice versa. The longer that I procrastinate, the worse my overall day will be because of the time and energy that I lost worrying about something.

I've found taking care of the dreaded item first invariably improves the rest of my day. When I get past something that I'm worried about, I know I've successfully taken care of the worst thing likely to happen to me all day. That accomplishment gives me a sense of optimism which improves my outlook. Your outlook can become a self-fulfilling prophecy. If your dread of a phone call is given enough time, it will color your outlook, and all too often the entire day becomes a bad one. On the other hand, the bump I get when I cross that dreaded item off my to-do list first thing often results in a more productive day.

Be intentional about the things to stay involved in and the things to let go of. It's always tempting to micromanage an organization you head because you care so much about the results. You know exactly what you want to happen, how it should be done, and if you don't say something it'll rarely be done exactly the way you believe it should have been done. However, there are several downsides to a micromanaging leadership style. For example, your people never develop—and if they're the type of people that you want, eventually they'll leave to go somewhere else where they will be allowed to develop. You also limit your organization's potential if you create an environment where you effectively make every major decision because there are only so many hours in the day and, therefore, only so much that you can take on.

I don't mean to say you should adopt the opposite extreme and become a hands-off manager. A manager who lets the organization run itself is not only abdicating their responsibility, they're guaranteeing that the organization will never fulfill its Vision. As I've discussed, an organization needs discipline to reach any worthwhile Vision. That discipline frequently requires making and implementing difficult decisions. When an organization is allowed to run itself, it's far more likely to take the easy route versus the difficult one. The easy route is never the right one when you're striving to achieve a Vision.

You should not only find a balance between micromanaging your organization and letting it run itself, you should be intentional about doing so. Take my steakhouse example. There are numerous things that go into a successful restaurant. You need professionally-appearing people in the front of the house taking good care of your customers and setting the tone for their visit, as well as hardworking, talented people in the kitchen preparing the meals. Someone must oversee the purchases and manage the inventory. Someone must keep the books. There's also payroll, accounts payable, and human resources issues to consider. You cannot take on all of this yourself and still fulfill your Vision of having the best steakhouse in town. So, what should you do?

Begin by deciding where you can make the most impact on the steakhouse. If your strengths lie in the kitchen and you've got a good head waiter, but your chef is inexperienced, then limit yourself to spot-checking the front of the house. Let your head waiter train and supervise the wait staff. Focus your time on training the chef with the goal of transferring responsibility to him or her as they develop.

This goal can sound easier than it is, but as your organization grows, it becomes much more critical. When Wildcat Oil Tools started, I did almost everything. As Wildcat Oil Tools grew, we added people and they took over some of the things that I had been doing. There were responsibilities that I was happy to let go off, such as delivering tools to locations, because I never learned how to back up a trailer properly. There were other things that were more difficult to let go of. When we started hiring salesmen, I had to let them do their job by contacting our customers. I've always enjoyed interacting with our customers and it was tempting to stay involved, but I couldn't do their jobs and mine.

The process of transitioning is a continual one. Organizations grow and change. You have to do likewise. As Wildcat Oil Tools continued to grow, our people became more specialized. Our accounting department is no longer one person who is responsible for every record and data entry. We've divided up the duties and responsibilities both in response to the volume of work and to provide better internal control. Our sales department has grown from one person to several individuals who are organized along customer, geographical, and product lines. This continued growth and specialization means I delegate more responsibility today than I did two years ago; and two years from now, I'll delegate even more. What's more, two years from now my job duties will have evolved even further. For example, our growth has brought with it problems that we didn't have a few years ago, such as international legal and financial issues as well as technology research and development issues.

I try to develop with our organization by focusing my efforts on the general strategic issues and emerging problems. I use the balance of my time to spot-check operational issues. As we continue to grow, my goal is to develop our people and let them take over more and more responsibility so that I can concentrate on the areas where I can best serve the organization.

Give yourself deadlines. All of us procrastinate at times and we fail to prioritize our projects properly by spending too much time on the things we enjoy and too little on the necessary chores. If a to-do list isn't your thing, another good way to avoid procrastinating is with deadlines. If I have three projects, assigning each a deadline ensures that I start work on the one that is most immediate in need rather than the one I would most rather do. This strategy also helps me avoid procrastination. When I was in school, knowing I had a big test in the morning was a sure way to focus my mind on studying the night before. I can accomplish the same thing if I commit myself to completing a project by the end of the day.

A deadline works in a similar way as a to-do list for me because I find myself automatically avoiding the inevitable distractions—emails, text messages, and the like, to meet a deadline. In fact, a pressing deadline often helps me put the phone away till I finish what I'm working on. I have a process in place to make sure if someone truly needs to get ahold of me, they can; but too often I, like most people, am prone to look at the phone every time it buzzes, rattles, or pings. The vast majority of the time, what it's alerting us to isn't urgent and we'd be far more efficient to let it wait until the important work is accomplished.

For deadlines to work, they must be reasonable, but short-term. So, what does a reasonable deadline mean? Assume it's Monday morning and you learn you've got to put together material for a client presentation that's scheduled for the end of next week. If you say to yourself, "I'll make my deadline 5:00 p.m. today," subconsciously you know you've got more time than that, and thus it'll be easy to procrastinate or allow yourself to become distracted. If, on the other hand, you determine how much time it will take to get the material together, you check for other conflicts, and you give the others in your organization the time they need to review your material before the presentation, you can set a deadline that your subconscious mind knows is real and you'll act accordingly.

What about short-term? My tax return is normally due April 15th. There is no point in me sitting down in October and setting deadlines for when I'll do my part to get this return prepared because a reasonable deadline would be months away and, therefore, I'd ignore it. I try to focus on things that I can accomplish in the next two to four weeks. Your situation or personality may require a longer or short period. That's fine. Just stick with a time period that consistently modifies your behavior.

Be selective with your deadlines. If you try to set deadlines for everything, the process becomes unworkable and you'll stop using it. Instead, pick out the most important thing, or the most important two or three things that absolutely have to be done in the near term, and then give yourself a deadline.

Finally, pick a system for recording and monitoring your deadlines. I depend on my Outlook calendar because that's what I use for all my scheduling and I have it on my computer and on my phone. Plus, it allows me to set reminders, so that I'm prompted as the deadline approaches.

Avoid unnecessary meetings. Face-to-face meetings are invaluable—when they're needed. For example, I'd much rather have personal contact with a customer than send a text or an email, and Wildcat Oil Tools uses periodic group meetings as a way of keeping the people in our various offices connected. Too often, however, meetings are unnecessary and wasteful. I've seen organizations fall into patterns and habits when it comes to meetings. For example, a particular

CHAPTER 15

group gets together every week or every month at an appointed day and time. Originally, there was probably a good reason for it but over time the group continues meeting at the appointed time because that's what they've grown accustomed to doing.

In my experience, getting a group together to discuss an issue when there isn't an obvious need results in an inordinate amount of time being spent accomplishing too little. Just as storage space seems to attract junk, having a scheduled meeting encourages the participants to discuss something. In the absence of a real agenda, that discussion will get sidetracked.

Thus, before scheduling a meeting, ask yourself, "Why this meeting and couldn't it be handled with a conference call, email chain, or text message?" If the meeting is appropriate, you'll have a quick and logical response. If you don't have one, then don't schedule a meeting, send an email, text, or make a call.

Get up early. I get up early in part because I like to work out before work. That physical activity gets me jump-started and I arrive at the office alert and focused. However, the mere fact that I'm an early riser in and of itself benefits me as a leader. Invariably, the stories that I've seen of successful leaders includes a reference to them being an early riser. I realize there are plenty of successful night owls as well. But when it comes to leaders, I'm convinced you need to become an early riser because as the old saying goes, "The early bird gets the worm." That's definitely true in the business world because opportunities are sometime fleeting and they may be gone before the night owl gets in gear.

Early risers get to work earlier than others. That gives them an opportunity to get ahead of the day. Walking into the office before 8:00

a.m. means walking into an office that hasn't already been inundated with phone calls and visitors. There's a relaxed atmosphere that gives you a chance to take the initiative and plan the day's activities. The time you spend working before the phone starts ringing, visitors begin dropping by, and the emails come flying in, is productive time because you're able to focus on the task at hand. But if you walk in at nine or ten o'clock, odds are your first tasks will be responding to outside events and, in fact, you may never gain control of your time.

Beginning your day in response-mode guarantees an inefficient day, because it prevents you from pre-planning or prioritizing beyond deciding who to respond to first. Real emergencies require emergency action, but not everyone else's emergency is necessarily your emergency. It's sometimes hard to recognize the difference when you're confronted with a situation just as you walk in the door. In my experience, if you begin the day in response-mode, you generally spend the rest of the day in response-mode. Even if you do get caught up before the day's gone, you're drained and unable to completely focus on anything.

I've also found when I start the day earlier, I finish the day earlier, which allows me more time for family and personal activities, and it helps me sleep better because it facilities a regular routine and it allows me some time to unwind. When I have to work late and then try to go to sleep shortly thereafter, I have a hard time turning off my mind. The experience is like that of being stuck on a treadmill and being unable to get off.

Don't skip breakfast. We've all heard breakfast is the most important meal of the day. I'm not sure if that was developed by the people who sell cereal or by medical professionals. I do know, however, if I skip breakfast I'm not nearly as energetic and focused as I am otherwise, and that I start to drag well before lunch. I keep a supply of protein shakes at my office. If I don't have time to sit down to a regular meal, I'll at least grab one of those. Healthy snacks, such as dried fruit, also work for me.

Let go at the end of the day. I saved this tip for last for several reasons. Obviously, it's the last thing you do each day and so it makes sense to talk about the importance of things like breakfast, getting to work early, and staying organized first. Plus, if you'll follow my tips to take care of the day's activities, you'll find it much easier to let go at the end of the day.

Nonetheless, letting go at the end of the day is still a worthy topic because all of us will have days where we seemingly can't let go and many regularly find it difficult to do so. If you fall into that latter category, I encourage you to go back over the tips in this chapter to see if there are areas where you could change your lifestyle. If, for example, you don't regularly work out now, I'm confident that starting a workout program that you enjoy, and not one that you view as a pure chore, will immediately improve your ability to leave the office at the office.

For all of us, the end of the day is a great example of the adage, "He who fails to plan, plans to fail." If you simply say to yourself, beginning tomorrow, "I'm committing myself to leaving business problems at the office," your mind will be like the new dog that is taken to the front yard and is told to stay. With nothing to keep it in place, and plenty of distractions in sight, the dog will be gone in seconds. To leave the office at the office, you need to focus on a routine that allows you to unwind and which minimizes the triggers that cause you to revisit the day's issues.

For me, the routine begins at the office with actions that tell my brain the workday is over. Think of going to a movie. At the end of the movie there's a musical score that replaces the dialogue and the camera fades away from the actors to a wider or different perspective, followed by the credits. When the credits roll, you know the story is over and it's time to gather your stuff and head toward the lobby. I want to feel a similar sensation when I leave the office.

There are numerous ways to accomplish this. Pick one that works for you. I, for one, like to put away whatever I was working on. I don't mean simply stacking up the papers and sliding them to the corner of my desk. I mean picking everything up, putting it in a file, putting the file in a drawer, closing the drawer, and turning out the lights as I leave my office. This simple act works for me because I find myself automatically shifting my focus from the day's problems to what I intend to do after I leave the office. Others could consider finishing some small task, such as responding to an email, just before you leave, or perhaps making a to-do list for tomorrow.

Whatever your "This is the end of my workday" task, you also need a "This is the start of my night" task. Maybe it's calling or texting home to say you're on the way, turning the car radio to a specific channel, or taking off your work shoes and putting on exercise shoes. There's no magic to the act; it simply needs to be one that your mind recognizes as a switch.

Finally, it helps me to focus on something positive when I first get home. If you have children, there's nothing like asking them about their day to get a totally non-work-related conversation going. Otherwise, asking your spouse about their day, having a glass of wine, or watching something like ESPN, will get your mind focused

CHAPTER 15

on something besides the day's problems. When your family asks you about your day, don't let yourself fall into the trap of reliving the day's problems. Unless it's something they can help you with, a short "it was fine" followed by a question directed to them, will prevent your mind from wandering.

CHAPTER SIXTEEN

ENCOURAGING INITIATIVE

I want people who can, and will, think for themselves. First off, I can't imagine effectively running a company if you have to tell everyone what to do, when to do it, and how to do it every step of the way. Secondly, I need problem-solvers because I can't be everywhere at once. Third, almost all of our people know more about their job than I do. That's one of the reasons we hired them. Fortunately, I've never had trouble hiring people who knew more than I did about their jobs, and then delegating responsibility to them. I've seen people bemoan the fact that their employees never think for themselves, while in the next breath, they berate someone who did something differently from what they would have done. Despite this management style, they don't realize this type of criticism is why their people are hesitant to exercise any initiative. The fact that these executives can't see they themselves are the source of their problem is both comical and sad. Micromanagement is a problem that you not only want to avoid, rather, you want to make sure you're encouraging the people in your organization to exercise initiative.

The good news is that initiative is in our country's DNA. The people who got on boats to emigrate to America were, by definition, capable of making independent decisions and taking personal risks. Those who couldn't stayed home. That initiative played an important part in our country's early history. It takes a special group of people to undertake a revolution against the world's strongest military and then implement an untried form of government.

I didn't serve in the military, but several of our employees have served. They tell me that the US military emphatically emphasizes personal initiative. At first blush, that sounds counter-intuitive. When I think of the military, I think of strict discipline and following orders without question. For example, you don't storm a machine gun nest if you aren't committed to the principle of following orders without thinking. Our military veterans tell me the military also teaches leadership at every level and that an important part of this training is encouraging people to exercise initiative and solve problems. One part of this training is treating someone who was confronted with a problem, and who then made a bad decision but nonetheless acted, differently from someone who failed to act at all. I'm told that it's far better to have a drill sergeant yelling at you for bad judgment than to having one yell at you for not exercising initiative. Both instances sound like yelling to me, but I'll take our company's former servicemembers' word for it.

When small unit military leaders are empowered to exercise initiative, it makes our military more unpredictable and therefore, harder for our enemies, particularly those who emphasize top-down decision making, to counter. In the business world, when your people exercise initiative, it makes your organization better at solving problems, taking care of customers, and seizing opportunity. Letting employees exercise initiative also results in a happier workforce because managers have more time to do their jobs and employees feel appreciated.

Do you encourage initiative? Here's a quick test: what did you do the last time someone made a decision without asking you and then did something differently from what you would have done? The people that I know who have control issues tend to criticize in this instance. If you work for them, it quickly becomes difficult to make an independent decision because not only do you have to analyze the problem, you must correctly predict what the boss would have done in this instance; and if you make a mistake, you get criticized. There are no future-predicting crystal balls, so no one can ever perfectly foresee the boss's reaction. It's safer to avoid deciding until you can let the boss decide for you.

Does that attitude mean you have simply to bite your tongue if the person who did something differently made a mistake? Of course not. Mistakes should be corrected so that they aren't repeated. But keep in mind two things: performing a task differently from the way you would have performed it isn't automatically a mistake; and you can simultaneously encourage the exercise of initiative and provide ongoing training to avoid the same mistakes, or similar ones, in the future.

For example, assume a customer has an issue about one of your products or services. Your employee meets with the customer and offers to discount the outstanding invoice and the cost of their next order in an effort to placate them and keep their business. Assume further that working with customers is part of the employee's job and that you have no policies or procedures in place prohibiting discounts in this situation. However, you don't want to use discounts to solve this type of problem because of unintended consequences. The boss with control issues will berate the employee for offering a discount and that employee, and anyone else who hears about the incident, will be far less likely to stick their neck out in the future to work with an unhappy customer. Instead, they'll be noncommittal and will let the boss decide what to do. How long do you think customers, who are already aggravated, will continue using a vendor if its sales staff isn't responsive? In addition how effective can a CEO be if he or she not only has to do their job, but has to make everyone else's decisions for them?

You, however, can avoid this situation while simultaneously training your staff. First, you sit down with the employee and you tell them that you appreciate the fact that they met with the customer and that they tried to resolve the problem because it's important that the organization be responsive to customers. Then you calmly explain why you don't like to offer discounts in this situation and what they might consider if they encounter this situation again. Finally, you reaffirm your appreciation for their efforts. If this is a good employee, they'll continue working with customers and looking for solutions, but will make better-informed decisions in the future.

There are several other ways that you can encourage people to exercise initiative. For example, make sure your managers include their staff when they set goals and develop action plans. Keep people informed about deadlines, supply issues, and other problems that impact their areas of work. If people have a good idea of what is going on in the organization and what you want to achieve, they're better equipped to solve problems.

Listen to staff members' ideas. You don't have to implement all of them but if people understand you're listening to their ideas and are interested in their suggestions, they're more likely to look for solutions. Give people credit and recognition when you do implement one of their ideas. That positive feedback will encourage everyone else to look for additional solutions.

There's one more reason for listening to your employees: they may be right. Your frontline personnel will have a different prospective from yours. As I've noted earlier, when we first started Wildcat Oil Tools, I knew everything because I was there for everything. When we started growing, I spent less time in the field and more time in my office and in my customers' field offices. Today, I rarely get to go to the field and even when I'm with a customer, it's probably in their boardroom or home office. My senior managers have similar issues. As a result, our frontline personnel know things that we don't. That knowledge may save you from a bad idea or produce a solution that you wouldn't have otherwise discovered.

CHAPTER SEVENTEEN

BRANDING

Throughout this book, I've discussed how you can lead your organization with a Vision and an Implementation Plan and thereby differentiate yourself from the competition through outstanding performance. I've saved for last a way to ensure your distinction is recognized. I've saved this step, not because it isn't important—in fact it's critically important—but because you need to have a solid foundation in place before this works. That step is branding your organization.

Branding is a general concept that can mean different things. For my purposes, I'll use the American Marketing Association's definition of brand: "A name, term, design, symbol, or any other feature that identifies one seller's goods or services as distinct from those of other sellers." If you're a non-profit, you might be tempted to say this doesn't apply to you, but if I asked you to visualize someone standing next to a kettle ringing a bell, what do you want to bet we'd both have the same basic image and that we'd associate it with the same organization? Still not convinced? How does a small child, too young to read, know that a sign with a large yellow "M" means french fries and an indoor playground?

You want a logo that becomes identified with your organization and that, when seen, causes people to think positively of you. Obviously, it would be nice to have something as widely recognized as the Salvation Army or McDonald's logo, but a successful brand need only be something that your customers, patrons, or donors recognize and associate with you. Your brand can be almost anything. Logos are one option and for most organizations are your best bet. There are, however, options. For example, Coca-Cola developed a customized bottle shape that most people recognize instantly. If you're a college sports fan, you associate colors or color combinations, hand signs, and sayings with particular teams. If you're a Harry Potter fan, a few musical notes from John Williams' film score will cause you to recall the movies and stories.

When you consider your brand, keep in mind several practical pointers. First, what do you want your brand to convey? The Nike swoosh is an excellent example of a logo that fits its business. The simple swoosh design conveys a sense of speed and motion—great attributes for a running shoe. Today, we automatically associate the swoosh with Nike without even thinking about it and we think nothing of spending more for a premium running shoe because we believe they're worth more. In 1971, however, when the company transitioned from simply importing running shoes to selling their own, Nike needed a design that was not only unique but one that helped convince customers to pay for premium running shoes.

Today that notion sounds obvious but in 1971 most people, including competing athletes, wore basic shoes for running. Nike,

CHAPTER 17

therefore, had an uphill battle to convince people that its shoes were worth a premium price. Phil Knight worked with Carolyn Davidson, a graphic design student at Portland State University, to create a logo to place on Nike's shoes. He asked her to make sure the logo conveyed motion and didn't look like Adidas' three-stripe design. She created several designs and presented them to Nike's management. The swoosh design was chosen.

Today, Nike's swoosh is one of the most valuable logos in the world. It's easily recognizable, it's well known, and is viewed favorably by most people. It's also grown with the company. Although the logo was originally used on shoes, today you can find the swoosh on a variety of objects including clothing, backpacks, watches, and water bottles. Each of these uses is consistent with fitness. Nike has reinforced this connection between its logo and fitness by utilizing several high-profile athletes as endorsers. Nike hopes to create a positive emotional attachment to the athlete, which will transfer that attachment to Nike's gear and clothing.

Nike's commercial success is proof that they've successfully convinced us that premium running shoes are worth the extra money. Their successful use of the swoosh on a wide variety of other athletic gear and equipment, most of which costs more than comparable generic products, is proof that they've expanded the value of their logo. Today, when you see the Nike logo on athletic equipment or apparel, most people have a positive image associated with fitness and athletic success and, therefore, we perceive Nike's products as more valuable and attractive.

Getting back to my original question: What do you want your brand to convey? Think of your brand as a promise. For example, when we see a logo or brand that we recognize on an article of clothing, a car, or a beverage, we make a judgment about that product because of the image we associate with that brand or logo and we expect the product to be consistent with our image. Major companies spend hundreds of millions of dollars creating and reinforcing a positive emotional response to the sight of their brand or logo. Next time you watch television, pay attention to the commercials. How many commercials actually convey hard information about their product or service versus those which primarily paint a picture?

For example, consider Mercedes-Benz's commercials. I'll bet you've heard the slogan, "The best or nothing," and that you automatically associate it with Mercedes-Benz. I'll also bet you can't recall anything from those commercials involving the specific performance of a Mercedes-Benz vehicle or why that vehicle is quantifiably better than a comparable vehicle from another manufacturer. Nonetheless, the commercials are incredibly effective, because the slogan conveys the promise that Mercedes-Benz always utilizes the highest engineering standards for their vehicles and that there are no compromises for safety, design, or engineering. When you see Mercedes-Benz's symbol on a car, they want you to intuitively assume that it is a well-designed and well-built car and that you would be proud to own it.

You want to achieve a similar response when people see your brand or logo. Let's go back to my steakhouse example. Our goal is to have the best steakhouse in town. Consequently, deciding what promise we want our brand or logo to convey is easy: when you come to our restaurant, you will always receive first-class service, you will invariably be served the best steak in town, and you will enjoy that steak in a relaxed atmosphere.

CHAPTER 17

Your branding strategy generally should consider your target audience. For example, if your target audience is tech-savvy teenagers, your general strategy will, of necessity be different from a strategy for singles, working moms, or senior citizens. In a similar way, if your target audience is regional, rather than national or international, you'll alter your strategy accordingly. For example, if my target audience is limited to a single state or region, I'll incorporate that state or region in my message because I want to connect with my target audience. However, if my target audience is national, a state- or regionally-focused message limits my opportunities. If my target is international, my message must be one that people from a wide variety of backgrounds can understand. In our steakhouse example, we'll keep things simple by assuming our target audience is limited to people in our immediate geographical area.

I'm not an expert on designing logos. I know a good one when I see it, but I can't tell you how to design one. For example, I love the Wildcat Oil Tools logo, but I had nothing to do with designing it. When I took possession of the four BOPs from the people to whom I had loaned the purchase money, and with which I started Wildcat Oil Tools, they had a drawing of a wildcat's face that I liked, so I made sure I acquired the right to use that drawing when I took possession of the BOPs. That drawing ultimately became the centerpiece of Wildcat Oil Tools' logo.

The reality is that what you chose to use for your logo or brand isn't nearly as important as what you do with it. While I love our Wildcat Oil Tools design, there's nothing about a picture of a wildcat that would ordinarily cause one to think of an oil-and-gas service company. I probably could have used the same design as the logo for innumerable different types of business. The logo worked for us because of what we did with it and how we protected our brand.

Let's assume we've developed a logo for our restaurant involving cutlery and a butcher's block. We like it, it's unique from anything other restaurants are using, and the people that we trust have told us it's a well-designed logo. So, what do we do with it? Easy. First, put it everywhere that is consistent with our promise to provide superior food, service, and atmosphere; second, don't put it anywhere that isn't consistent with this promise; and third, make sure it looks the same every time we use it.

Ideally, you want to use the logo so widely that when people see it, they instantly associate it with you. So, we'll place our logo on the front door, the menus, our employee uniforms, our advertisements, our letterhead, our website, and so on. We've used our logo in a similar way at Wildcat Oil Tools. If you come to any Wildcat Oil Tools facility, you'll see our Wildcat Oil Tools logo on every truck, building, and uniform. If you go online, you'll see it in our social media posts and pictures, as well as on our website. We like to post pictures of our operations on social media sites such as LinkedIn and Facebook. Originally, we simply included pictures with our social media posts. However, one of our competitors copied some of our photos and then used them for their own posts. That appropriation's unbelievable, I know, but it happened. So now, when you see a picture on our social media posts, you'll see a Wildcat logo watermarked onto each post with Photoshop. I hoped our competitor would continue copying our pictures and using them in their posts, but unfortunately watermarking that stopped them.

CHAPTER 17

To return to our mythical steakhouse: achieving logo visibility is relatively easy because you can control how often the logo is used. The trick is protecting that logo so that it reinforces your promise to provide superior food, service, and atmosphere. The last thing you want is for people to see the logo and associate it with anything less than the highest quality. At Wildcat Oil Tools, I'm particular about our logo's use. At times, my vigilance probably drives people crazy; but there's a reason why I insist our logo look good every time it's used, and why I also insist the logo only be used on high-quality items.

When you see the Wildcat Oil Tools logo, I want you to think of first-class products and services. It's hard to make that association if you see our logo on a dirty, broken-down piece of equipment. Consequently, I'm a stickler about making sure our promotional items look first-class. How you reinforce your promise will vary widely depending on your product or service. For example, when you see the Nike swoosh on a well-worn t-shirt, that image reinforces your image of Nike as a provider of quality athletic equipment because you know that t-shirt has been through countless workouts and contests; and if we bought one, we could put it through the ringer too. If you replaced the swoosh with the Wildcat logo, however, you might think of the shirt as a cleaning rag, instead.

Consequently, if I oversaw Nike's marketing, I'd continue using the swoosh on t-shirts and similar workout clothing and I'd be excited when I saw it on well-worn clothing. For Wildcat Oil Tools, however, I insist our logo only go on quality polo and button-down shirts. First, I want to use our logo on clothing that people want to wear. But more importantly, when you see our logo on a shirt, I want you to think—even if only subconsciously—that it's a nice shirt.

I'm also a stickler for keeping our trucks and equipment clean. If you drove past one of our yards and saw an exceptionally dirty truck parked out front, you'll probably assume it's not well-maintained. On the other hand, I could take a truck that isn't even operable, clean it up, give it a fresh paint job, park it out front, and you'd make the opposite assumption. Appearances matter. Consequently, when you see the Wildcat Oil Tools logo on a truck, I want that truck's appearance to scream "well-maintained." That isn't easy in the oilfield, because we drive a lot of miles on dirt roads. For us, it's even more challenging because our trucks are black. But when they're clean, those trucks look sharp. Our customers know and appreciate how difficult it is to keep a black truck clean in the oilfield. When they see we take care of our trucks consistently, they're inclined to assume we take the same care with all our equipment—and they're right to do so, because we do. Seeing the Wildcat Oil Tools logo on those well-maintained trucks leads to a connection between our logo and superior products and services.

We can do the same thing in our steakhouse. Earlier I suggested putting the logo on things such as the front door, menus, and employee uniforms. Each of these places would be a logical place to use a logo, but before you do, take another look at each. Are they consistent with your promise to provide superior steaks, service, and atmosphere? If not, I'd strongly suggest that you upgrade those places immediately. Next, verify that the logo looks good on each item. A logo should look consistent across every platform, but that doesn't mean you can use the same PDF file in every instance. If the logo doesn't look good on a sample, find out why and fix it. In the hustle and bustle of today's business world, it's sometimes easy to say, "Close enough is good enough," but when it comes to branding, you must be a stickler and a perfectionist every time.

I mentioned I don't use the Wildcat Oil Tools logo on inexpensive t-shirts because of my concern that an inexpensive t-shirt is inconsistent with the image we want to project. Given the promise that we want our steakhouse logo to convey, there will be things that you don't want to put the logo on. For example, I probably wouldn't use it on cleaning towels or anything else that our customers wouldn't characterize as high-quality.

Logos are important to branding, but you can't stop there. Everything that we do in connection with the restaurant must be consistent with our promise. Our employees are responsible for almost all our customer interactions; consequently, it's important that they be aware of, and periodically reminded of, our promise because their actions must discharge that promise. This requires you be aware not only of how they should perform but how they do perform in every aspect of the business. For example, when a customer walks in the door, is what they see and what they hear from our employees consistent with our promise? The same holds true for every portion of their experience until they pull out of the parking lot.

At Wildcat Oil Tools, I developed policies and procedures to ensure our employees knew what to do and how to do it, because I wanted everything that we did to reflect my Vision of building a world-class service company. You'll need to do something similar because you can't expect your employees to consistently meet expectations unless they know what those expectations are and are trained on how to meet them. This will require a lot of time and effort on your part because the attention to detail makes all the difference in the world. Next time you're in a nice restaurant, closely watch a good waiter or waitress at work. There's a pattern to how they do everything, from whom they address first and how they do so, how they take down and confirm your order, how they deliver and pick up plates and glasses, all the way to how they handle the customer's bill. This pattern is the result of training and supervision.

A solid training program is essential to any well-run organization. To develop one for your organization, you'll need to start with your Vision and work backward. Ask yourself: What would an organization that fulfills the Vision look like? How would that organization act and perform? What would the key members of the organization be capable of doing? Then take those answers and develop the procedures that, when followed, will achieve your Vision.

Here's an example of how that would work at our steakhouse. When a group is seated, we want the table's appearance to stand out. So, you develop a table setup procedure that will be used every time. That procedure would include instructions on what will be put on the table, where, and in some instances how. Your employees would know, for example, where to put the different types of beverage glasses and how to arrange them, what silverware to set out and where, and where to put the main dinner plate and any smaller plates. Our procedure would also provide instructions on handling items. For example, how to pick up glasses by the stem and cutlery from the middle to eliminate fingerprints; what pattern to use when folding napkins; and how and when to open and present the menu to customers.

CHAPTER 17

As you can see, this process necessarily involves a lot of detail, but invariably it's the little things that separate superior organizations from their competition. And when developing your brand, the little things are essential. If we hire the best cooks, buy the best cuts of meat, and use first-class cooking equipment, we can cook the best steak in town. However, if we don't also provide superior service, we'll never be known as the best steakhouse in town. Instead when people see our logo, they'll think that's the restaurant with great food but.... Our Vision doesn't allow for a "but" and, therefore, our procedures should eliminate them. I guarantee you that the time you put in developing and implementing quality control procedures, assuming you consistently follow them, will create a brand of which you can be proud, and one that will separate you from the competition.

CONCLUSION

I hope you enjoy reading this book as much as I've enjoyed working on it. The process brought back a lot of fond memories about Wildcat Oil Tools' early days, reminded me not only of how far we've come but the contributions so many made to make our success possible. I'm proud of the team that we've assembled and of what we've accomplished so far. I look forward to working with them as we continue the pursuit of making Wildcat Oil Tools a world-class oil and gas technology and service company.

I have no doubt that if you'll consider the leadership lessons in this book and apply them to your organization, you'll create an organization committed to creating and offering a world-class product/service that can achieve wonders. It will take work, discipline, and the right Mindset but at the end of the day, every minute you spend in pursuit of your Vision will be well worth the effort.

The good news is you're perfectly capable of putting this strategy to work. There are some things in life that may require innate talent. For example, if you want to be a professional athlete or entertainer, your parent's genealogy is important. Anyone, however, can make themselves a better leader. And with the right Vision, Plan, and Mindset, you can make your organization stand out from its peers.

Good luck with your journey!

ABOUT THE AUTHOR

Aron Marquez is an entrepreneur. His first business was a lawn mowing service that he started with a friend. Today he is the CEO of Wildcat Oil Tools, an international oilfield service company, and has started Flecha Azul Tequila, a top-shelf tequila company, and Black Quail Apparel, an active wear apparel company.

ACKNOWLEDGMENTS

Wildcat Oil Tools' success is the story of countless contributions by numerous people, but it begins with my parents. I owe everything that I've accomplished to the sacrifices they made to make sure my siblings and I had what we needed, the guidance they provided us as we grew up, and the love they've always shown us.

Wildcat Oil Tools is a success story because of our people. Their commitment to each other and our vision made this story possible. This book contains several stories to illustrate their commitments and the inspiration they provided. I wish that I could have included more and promise to do so in my next book. Until then, I want everyone who has worked with and for Wildcat Oil Tools to understand how much I have treasured our shared experiences and how much I look forward to facing tomorrow's challenges with you.

Finally, I want to thank our General Counsel, Rick Strange, for his help. This book was a collaborative effort on our parts. I couldn't have done this without his help.

www.ingramcontent.com/pod-product-compliance
Lightning Source LLC
Chambersburg PA
CBHW031626160426
43196CB00006B/293